Indonesian Cookery

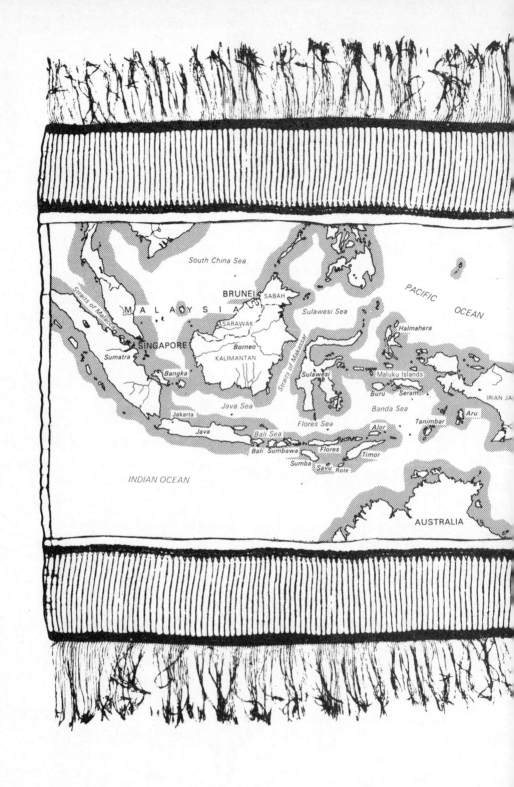

David Scott and Surya Winata

*I*ndonesian *C*ookery

Illustrated by Steve Hardstaff
from photographs by David Scott

Rider
London Melbourne Sydney Auckland Johannesburg

Also by David Scott

The Japanese Cookbook
Recipes for Living
Grains, Beans, Nuts
Middle Eastern Vegetarian Cookery
Traditional Arab Cookery

Rider & Company

An imprint of the Hutchinson Publishing Group
17–21 Conway Street, London W1P 6JD

Hutchinson Publishing Group (Australia) Pty Ltd
PO Box 496, 16–22 Church Street, Hawthorne, Melbourne,
Victoria 3122

PO Box 151, Broadway,
New South Wales 2007

Hutchinson Group (NZ) Ltd
32–34 View Road, PO Box 40–086, Glenfield, Auckland 10

Hutchinson Group (SA) Pty Ltd
PO Box 337, Bergvlei 2012, South Africa

First published 1984
© David Scott 1984
Illustrations © Steve Hardstaff 1984

Set in Linotron Bembo by Wyvern Typesetting Ltd, Bristol

Printed in Great Britain by The Anchor Press Ltd
and bound by Wm Brendon & Son Ltd, both of Tiptree, Essex

British Library Cataloguing in Publication Data
Scott, David
Indonesian cookery
I. Cookery, Indonesian
I. Title II. Winata, Surya
641.59598 TX724.5.15

ISBN 0 09 155401 2

AUTHOR'S NOTE

This book was written by David Scott with the collaboration of Surya Winata. David Scott, who is an author and restauranteur, spent time in Indonesia with Surya Winata, proprietor of the Kebayoran Inn and Vic's Viking Restaurant in Jakarta, and from this friendship this book developed. Surya provided the basic information and expertise, while David selected and adapted the recipes and presented the material in a way suited to the Western cook.

The authors would like to thank Geoffrey Chesler, our editor, for his support, creativity and keen wit, all important ingredients in the enjoyable production of this book. We would also like to thank John Bunton for introducing us to each other, with our common interest in cookery in mind.

CONTENTS

INTRODUCTION

Indonesia, although it is a huge country made up of thousands of islands which vary from one group to another in respect of climate and habitat, does have an underlying basic identity. This is reflected in the cuisine which has a distinctive style that unifies the various local cuisines, themselves counterpointed by the special local availability of particular ingredients.

Apart from national influences, Indonesian cooking has assimilated the influence of various foreign cultures. Initially it was from the Chinese whose people traded with and emigrated to Indonesia for thousands of years. Later, from the fourth century AD, Indian invaders and tradesmen brought with them Hindu, Buddhist and, most important, Muslim ideas and attitudes. This Arab influence was reinforced by visiting Arab scholars and merchants and by Indonesians who had been on pilgrimages to Mecca. Last, and possibly of least importance as regards national cuisine, was the Dutch invasion of Indonesia in the sixteenth century.

Thus we have a cooking style that, together with the natural Indonesian sense of colour, presentation and individual flair, has absorbed the Chinese respect for quality and for retaining the intrinsic properties of each ingredient, and the Indian and Arabic skill in the use of fragrances and spices. Together they produce a unique and exciting style of cuisine which is well expressed in the motto of the Indonesian coat of arms. The motto is held in the claws of the mythical eagle-like bird, the garuda, carrier of the Lord God Vishnu. It says 'Bhinneka Tunggal Ika' which means 'Unity in Diversity'.

INDONESIAN FOOD AND CUSTOMS

Indonesia, by virtue of its climate and rich volcanic soil, is a fertile land. Rice, fruits and vegetables are grown in great variety and abundance. It is a country made up of many islands, and sea fish and shell fish of all sorts are readily available, both fresh and dried. Freshwater fish are caught in the rivers and inland lakes and are also bred by rice farmers in their flooded paddy fields. Meat is expensive for the majority of the people and, although still popular, is eaten in much smaller quantities than in the West. It is never served as a steak or joint but cut into small cubes or thin slices, or minced. The meat is fried or grilled and served in, or with, a sauce. Lamb is possibly the most common and most popular meat, followed by beef. Pork is forbidden to the Muslim community but it is enjoyed by the Chinese and the Hindus, particularly on Bali, where the characteristic Balinese pig seems to have the free run of the streets, except when in a basket on the way to market. Many Indonesian families outside the towns keep chickens and ducks. The chickens run free and their flesh is tasty if sometimes on the tough side. The ducks are kept in flocks and are herded to the fields each morning where they spend the day swimming and feeding in the irrigation canals of the paddy fields.

Throughout Indonesia many festivals are held to celebrate the various climatic and farming cycles of the year. They express the intrinsic respect for nature and its potential for good or evil that is part of the animism which underlies all the religions of Indonesia. These occasions, together with the numerous religious feasts (Muslim, Hindu, Buddhist and Christian) are accompanied by the preparation of much food, some of which will be offered to the gods. Great care goes into the making of this food and this same attitude is carried over into the preparation of everyday meals, which are invariably presented as attractively as possible. Even the lowliest of dishes is brightened up by a little garnish of chopped herbs or grated coconut or fried onion flakes.

A normal Indonesian meal will consist of rice plus a variety of side dishes, all served together. The side dishes of vegetables, poultry, fish and/or meat are accompanied by hot spicy sauces or relishes called sambals, soya sauce (the sweet and the salty varieties) and a simple fresh salad. The basic flavouring, seasoning and thickening agents used by the cook are chillies, small shallot-style onions, lemon or lime juice, ginger root, cumin, coriander, turmeric, grated or desiccated coconut and coconut milk. The milk is not the liquid inside a coconut which in Indonesia is called coconut water, but the milky liquid which is made by pressing through a sieve grated or desiccated coconut which has been soaked in water.

At the dining table the rice is placed in the centre, surrounded by all the other dishes and, if guests are present, more food than could possibly be eaten is presented as a mark of hospitality. The food is eaten from a plate or banana leaf with a spoon (the implement taken to the mouth) and fork (used to load the spoon) or fingers, using only the right hand. Finger bowls are provided for those deft enough to eat with their fingers, which is not too difficult when the rice is sticky and the other foods are already cut into mouth-sized portions. Drinks served with the meal could be plain water, sweet tea (no milk), black coffee, beer or fruit juice. Incidentally, for cooling your mouth after eating hot chillies, a piece of cucumber is much better than a glass of cold water. The meal usually ends with fresh fruit and a pot of hot, strong coffee and sugar. It is called kopi tubruk (collision coffee) because the boiling water is poured directly onto the grains of coffee. Desserts and puddings as we know them in the West are served as snacks between meals.

COOK'S NOTES

The recipes chosen for this book have been selected to give a real taste of Indonesian food within the limits of a Western kitchen. As with other foreign styles of cooking, complete authenticity outside the country of origin is very difficult. Indonesian cooks, however, are proud of their individuality, and authenticity is more a question of style than of fine detail. It is best to approach Indonesian cooking bearing this attitude in mind.

Most of the ingredients used are readily available but where something uncommon is required, a good substitute is given in the recipe. The recipes can be prepared with only a moderate amount of skill and they introduce a style of cooking relatively unknown in the West (except in Holland which had colonial links with Indonesia), that has its own attractive and distinctive taste, texture and appearance. Perhaps the simplest description within reference points with which you may be familiar is that it combines some of the cooking methods of China with some of the spices of India and unites the two with a uniquely Indonesian style.

The following ingredients are required in many of the recipes, and it may be useful to have them available when using this book:

Vegetable oil

Peanuts, raw or roasted, crunchy peanut butter

Desiccated coconut

Soya sauce, both the dark and sweet and light and salty varieties, both available from Chinese grocery stores. (See glossary)

Brown sugar
Ginger, fresh or dried green root or powder
Garlic
Bay leaves
Cumin seeds
Coriander seeds
Black or white pepper
Chillies dried or fresh, chilli powder and hot pepper (chilli) sauce
Turmeric
Lemons or limes
White vinegar.

Herbs and flavourings that are difficult to obtain outside South East Asia or specialist food shops occur rarely in the recipes given here and where they do, alternatives have been given. For more details of particularly Indonesian ingredients refer to the glossary.

Spices

The most common way of using herbs and spices in Indonesian cookery is to grind the dry ingredients into a powder. Fresh ingredients such as chillies, garlic, ginger root, peanuts or herbs are then added to the spices and the mixture is ground to a paste. (For grinding methods see the section on equipment, page 17.) The paste is then fried in a little oil and the main ingredients of the dish are sautéed in it before cooking.

Coconut Milk

Coconut milk is not the liquid inside a coconut, which is called coconut water, it is the liquid pressed from grated coconut flesh diluted with water, or from desiccated coconut after it has been soaked in lukewarm water. Coconut milk is important in Indonesian cooking both as a flavouring and as a thickening agent. In the West it can be made from desiccated coconut and a recipe is given on page 15. Alternatively it can be bought canned in Chinese or Indian grocery stores. Use the unsweetened variety. In Indonesia, coconut milk is always made by grating fresh coconut flesh, soaking it in water and then pressing the liquid from it (see page 15). There are, strictly speaking, three grades of coconut milk used in cooking: thick, medium and thin. The category depends on whether the milk has been obtained from unpressed (thick), once pressed (medium-thick) or twice pressed (thin) grated coconut flesh. In this book when coconut milk is given in the ingredients it refers to the medium-thick milk prepared from either desiccated or freshly grated coconut. Or alternatively, it refers to canned unsweetened coconut milk.

To Prepare Coconut Milk from Desiccated Coconut

8 oz (225 g) desiccated coconut
1 pint (575 ml) water

Put the coconut in a pan and cover with lukewarm water. If you have a blender put the mixture in, blend for 20 seconds and then filter the contents through a muslin cloth or fine sieve, collecting the liquid. Press the resultant mush hard to remove the last residue of juice. This produces the medium-thick coconut milk which is required for the recipes in this book.

   If you do not have a blender, leave the coconut soaking in the water for 20 minutes and then squeeze and knead the mixture until it turns milky and filter. To make thin milk, repeat the above procedure, using the coconut mush in the sieve in place of the desiccated coconut. For very thick coconut milk (which is more appropriately called coconut cream) follow the above method but use half the volume of water.

To Prepare Coconut Milk from Fresh Coconut

1 fresh small coconut
12 fl oz (350 ml) water

Grate the flesh of the coconut into a bowl and add the water. Squeeze the flesh in the water for a minute or two to press out all the milk. Strain the liquid off, press the pulp to remove the last residue of juice. This is the medium-thick santan required for the recipes in this book.

Cooking with Coconut Milk

Fresh coconut milk from either freshly grated or desiccated coconut should be used within 8 hours of being made. Canned coconut milk will keep in the fridge for 1–2 days after opening. Once coconut milk has been added to a dish it should not be heated to more than a very gentle boil and the cooking pan or casserole dish containing the milk should not be covered. After adding the coconut milk stir the dish continuously up to boiling point then for at least 7 or 8 minutes afterwards. This ensures that the sauce is smooth and also prevents the milk from curdling or separating. Dishes cooked with coconut milk, if kept overnight, should be stored in the fridge.

Cooking Oils

Coconut oil, and to a lesser extent, margarine and ghee (prepared from goat fat) are the traditional Indonesian cooking fats. Sunflower seed oil, corn oil and peanut oil are all good substitutes.

Chillies

If you are cutting fresh chillies it is best to handle them wearing rubber gloves as they can irritate the skin. Do not touch your eyes with the gloves on. Wash the gloves immediately the job is finished. To reduce the fierceness of chilli peppers remove the seeds before chopping them and adding them to the dish. Alternatively, leave them to soak in cold water for an hour before adding them to the dish. You can also add them whole and remove them before serving.

Dried chillies are as hot as the fresh variety but because they contain no volatile oils they do not burn the skin as quickly. Red and green chillies are equally hot though there is no method of predicting the strength of a particular chilli, and even within the same batch some are hotter than others.

One teaspoon of hot pepper sauce used as a substitute for fresh or dried chillies is equivalent to 2 medium fresh or dried chilli peppers. Chinese-style hot pepper sauce, not the Mexican variety, is what is meant in the recipes in this book that contain chilli sauce. (See also the glossary for more information on chillies.)

Onions

Recipes have been tested using common white or brown onions and the following approximations have been used:

1 small onion is taken to weigh an average of 2 oz (50 g)
1 medium onion averages 4 oz (100 g)
1 large onion averages 8 oz (225 g)

Shallots are slightly closer in taste to the onions generally used in Indonesian cooking and if they are available and you wish to try them in the recipes, substitute 4 shallots for 1 medium-sized onion.

Chicken

To divide a chicken into portions for a curry or for other dishes in which small pieces are required, cut the chicken as follows: the leg into 2 pieces; the wing into 2 pieces; the back into 4 pieces; divide the breast down the centre and cut each half into 2 pieces.

Tamarind Water

2 oz (50 g) tamarind
4 fl oz (100 ml) water

To make tamarind water of the strength required for the recipes in this book, put the tamarind in a small stainless steel pan and add the water.

Press the soft pulp formed with the back of a spoon to squeeze out the juices and then pour the liquid and pulp into a strainer. Collect the liquid and press the pulp in the strainer to extract all the juices. Use the brown liquid, called tamarind water, collected, in the recipes as directed. Lemon juice can be used as a substitute in which case use the same quantity as you would if you were using tamarind water. (See glossary for more information on tamarind water.) Lemon rind mixed with a little vinegar can also be substituted.

Kecap Manis

If you find it hard to buy kecap manis you can make your own, using the following recipe.

2 oz (50 g) dark brown sugar
6 fl oz (150 ml) dark soya sauce

Dissolve the sugar in the soya sauce. Kecap manis is good sprinkled over boiled white rice.

Equipment

All the essential equipment for Indonesian-style cooking is available in a normal well-equipped kitchen, although there are a couple of non-essential items that either save time and energy or add to the authenticity of the cooking method. In the first category comes the blender or electric grinder, which is used to grind spices and other flavouring or thickening ingredients into a smooth paste. If you don't have a blender or grinder or if you only need to grind a small quantity of ingredients, then a heavy pestle and mortar or hand mill should be used. If using a pestle and mortar, crush the flavourings with a pressing, rolling motion rather than an up and down pounding action. Finally, if you don't have any grinding equipment, you can make a coarse paste by using ground spices and mixing them with a little oil and with the other ingredients very finely chopped. In the second category comes the main Indonesian cooking utensil, the wok. This is the curved bottomed, circular pan used in Chinese cooking. The wok is an excellent pan for quick frying, deep frying, sautéeing, simmering, in fact for all the different methods of cooking done on top of the stove. For use on a conventional hot plate, or gas ring, they need to be supported on a small metal frame but these can usually be purchased with the wok.

To season a new wok, wash it gently with some soapy water. Rinse well and then dry it over a low gas or electric hot plate. Add 2 fl oz (50 ml) of vegetable oil and 1 teaspoon of salt and heat it until it smokes. Swivel the pan about to cover all the inside surface with oil.

Remove it from the heat and pour the oil off. Allow the pan to cool and then rinse it with plain hot water. Dry off again and repeat the whole process. Finally, apply an oil coating over the inside surface of the pan and rub the excess oil off with a paper towel. After you've seasoned the wok never use detergent to wash it, just hot water and a soft, non-metal pad.

If you do not own a wok, nor wish to buy one, normal pots and frying pans are perfectly good for all the recipes given in this book.

Quantities and Menus

Indonesians usually serve 4 or 5 dishes and rice at one meal so it is difficult in a Western cookery book, when the user may wish to make only one dish, to gauge the quantities to be given in a particular recipe. I have decided to give recipes designed to serve about 4 people. The exceptions to this rule are indicated in the recipes concerned. Thus if you wish to provide 3 or 4 different dishes at one meal, choose the recipe and then halve the quantities given. You will then have enough food for about 6 people. The relative quantities given in the recipes, particularly of spices and herbs, can also be adjusted to suit personal taste, just as the Indonesian cook would adjust them.

To prepare a menu for an Indonesian meal select from the recipes one or more, depending on how elaborate the meal is to be, vegetable, seafood, meat, chicken or egg dish and serve them with plain rice or another rice dish and some or all of the following: a soup, a selection of sambal (hot sauces), a salad, savoury or sweet side dishes and fresh fruit.

Here are a number of suggested menus but do not let them discourage you from making up your own combinations. It's good fun and allows you to put your own distinctive stamp on each meal. To help you to do this, a list of all the recipes in this book is given in the index. Remember, in an Indonesian meal, all the dishes are served at the same time and the diners themselves choose in what order and in what combination to eat them.

White Rice (Nasi Putih)
Fried Chicken (Ayam Goreng)
Mixed Vegetables in Coconut Milk (Sayur Lodeh)
Eggs in Chilli and Tomato Sauce (Telur Belado)
Prawn Crackers (Krupuk Udang)

White Rice (Nasi Putih)
Mild Lamb or Mutton Curry (Gulai Kambing)
Mixed Vegetable Salad with Peanut Sauce (Gado-gado)
Fried Fish with Sweet Spicy Sauce (Ikan Goreng Bumbu Manis)
Savoury Peanut Fritters (Rempeyek Kacang)

Simple Fried Rice (Nasi Goreng)
Vegetable Curry (Kari Sayur)
Yellow Fried Fish (Ikan Bumbu Kuning)
Cucumber Pickle (Acar Ketimun)
Dry Roasted Peanuts (Kacang Goreng Kering)

White Rice (Nasi Putih)
Spiced Grilled Chicken (Singgang Ayam)
Curried Beef Sumatran Style (Gulai Sumatra)
Stir Fried Vegetables (Sayur Tumis)
Fish Soup (Soto Ikan)

Yellow Rice with Coconut Milk (Nasi Kuning)
Marinated Braised Beef in Soya Sauce (Lapis Daging)
Tamarind Fried Fish (Ikan Goreng)
Fried Bean Curd with Vegetables (Tahu Sayur Bumbu Kacang)
Curried Chicken Soup (Soto Ayam Bumbu Kari)
Prawn Crackers (Krupuk Udang)

Rice Cooked in Coconut Milk (Nasi Santan)
Stir Fried Carrot (Wortel Tumis)
Fish in Soya Sauce (Ikan Kecap)
Roasted Chicken in Marinade, Grilled (Ayam Panggang Kecap)
Corn Fritters (Perkedel Jagung)
Banana Fritters (Pisang Goreng)

White Rice (Nasi Putih)
White Curried Chicken (Opor Ayam)
Meatballs with Vegetable Soup (Sop Bakso)
Mixed Vegetable Salad with Coconut Sauce (Urap)
Fried Noodles with Beef and Prawns (Mi Goreng Sapi)

Special Fried Rice (Nasi Goreng Istimewa)
Beef Sate with Chilli Hot Peanut Sauce (Sate Sapi Bumbu Kacang Pedas)
Fried Spiced Pork Meatballs (Perkedel Babi Goreng)
Indonesian Fruit Salad (Rujak)
Spiced Fried Prawns (Udang Goreng Bumbu)

Sweet Smelling Coconut Rice (Nasi Gurih)
Lamb Sate with Mild Peanut Sauce (Sate Kambing Bumbu Kacang)
Spicy Beef Stew in Soya Sauce (Semur Daging)
Grilled Wrapped Fish (Ikan Pepes Bakar)
Braised Noodle (Mi Goreng Kuah)

Festive Rice Cone (Nasi Tumpeng)
Chicken in Lemon or Tamarind Marinade, Fried (Ayam Goreng Asam Garam)
Vinegared Mixed Vegetables (Acar Kuning)
Spiced Stuffed Fish, Baked (Ikan Isi)
Bamboo Shoots and Cabbage Soup (Sop Kol Rebung)
Seasoned and Fried Bean Curd (Tahu Bumbu Goreng)
Chilli Hot Lamb or Mutton Curry (Gulai Jawa)
Chicken Sate (Sate Ayam)

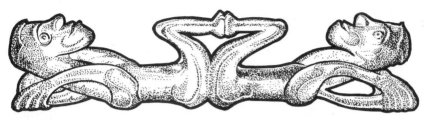

GLOSSARY OF INGREDIENTS

Asam	see *Tamarind*
Bamboo shoots	very young, tender bamboo shoots which are eaten as a vegetable. They are available ready cooked in tins at any Chinese grocery store
Bananas (pisang)	there are many varieties of banana in Indonesia. Some are cultivated for cooking and others for eating fresh. The best for cooking are called pisang kepok
Bean curd	see *Tahu*
Beansprouts	some dried beans, particularly soya and mung beans, can be sprouted to give tasty white shoots. Beansprouts have become well-known and easily available in the West. Nearly all the beansprouts seen in the shops are grown from mung beans
Blachan	see *Prawn paste*
Cabe rawit	see *chilli peppers*
Candlenuts (kemiri)	the kernel of this nut is waxy, hence its name. It is walnut sized and although originally a native plant of Australia, it is sometimes used in Indonesian cooking. Macadamia nuts are often used instead of candlenuts. Walnuts, brazil nuts or almonds are also sometimes substituted for candlenuts
Cardamom	an aromatic spice available as a seed or a pod. Black cardamom pods are stronger than green pods which are stronger than the sun-blanched white ones
Chilli peppers	chilli peppers are a regular ingredient of Indonesian food. The small (1/2in/1 cm) very hot variety called cabe rawit (known as bird's eye or bird chilli in the

West) and the longer, more familiar thin red or green types that are less hot are both used. Unless you are familiar with the searing hotness of chillies, I would not advise you to eat them raw or to even nibble at one. The Indonesian cook uses fresh or dried chillies and usually makes them into a paste by crushing them with a little salt in a pestle and mortar before using them. The paste, thinned with a small quantity of water, is the hot sauce called sambal ulek. You can buy it commercially or you can make your own by combining fresh or dried chillies, with seeds removed, with salt and water and grinding the mixture to a paste. Hot chilli or pepper sauce is an excellent substitute. (Incidentally, Indonesians call somebody intense with passion – love, hate, politics etc. – a *cabe rawit!*)

The hotness of chillies takes some getting used to but after you do, their beneficial qualities can be appreciated. In a hot climate, because they bring your body temperature closer to that outside, paradoxically you feel cooler. They also stimulate the appetite and to some extent purify suspect food. However, you must take care for addiction to chillies can lead to ulcers

Chinese cabbage   the two types of Chinese cabbage generally available in the West are used interchangeably in Indonesian cooking. One variety has long pale green stems and leaves and the other has long stems and green leaves. If neither are available, cos lettuce can be substituted

Cloves   ground and whole are used in cookery but they are perhaps best known for their use in flavouring kretek cigarettes. The smell of kretek, so called because they crackle when smoked, is found everywhere in Indonesia where people congregate. The cloves in kretek cigarettes help to cool the throat after a hot meal and Indonesians usually prefer them to American cigarettes

Coconut milk (santan)   see Cook's Notes

Coconut oil   coconuts are a staple crop in Indonesia and every part of them is put to good use. Coconut oil is the most commonly used cooking oil. It is not, however, essential to Indonesian cooking and a good quality vegetable oil can be substituted

Coconut water	this is the liquid inside the coconut that we, usually, wrongly call coconut milk. As the coconut ripens and gets older, the thin, transparent flesh coating the inner side hardens and slowly becomes the thick white flesh of the nut. The older the coconut, the less water there is and the less sweet it is. Young coconuts are sold at roadside stalls, in Indonesia, where the stall holder will slice the top off for you and stick a straw into the centre to allow you to drink the water. You then hand him the nut back, he slices it in two, chops a piece off the fibrous outer shell, shapes it into a wedge-shaped spoon and hands it back to you, together with the coconut halves so that you can scrape off the tender flesh and eat it
Coriander and cumin(ketumbar and jinten)	these two spices are invariably used together and they are possibly the most used spices (apart from chillies) in Indonesian cookery. For the best flavour buy the seeds and crush them yourself before use. Otherwise, use the ground variety. Fresh coriander leaves, if available, are used for garnishing
Curry leaves	from a tree native to South East Asia used fresh or dried in curries and powdered in the preparation of curry powder
Daun salem leaves	used extensively in Indonesian cookery for their flavour. Bay leaves can be substituted although they impart a slightly different taste
Ebi	see *Prawns, dried*
Ginger (jaher)	ginger root is indigenous to Indonesia and the young green fresh root is much used in cooking. The dried root available in the West is a fine substitute and, failing that, ground ginger can be used
Kecap	see *Soya sauce*
Ketan	glutinous rice usually prepared for making sweet dishes

Laos	a member of the ginger family. Not available in the West and not used in any of the recipes given in this book
Lemon grass (sereh, serai)	a long thin green grass used as a herb. Grated lemon rind can be substituted. Powdered sereh is occasionally stocked in herb or spice shops. Use it sparingly
Lime	used in Indonesian cooking in the same way as lemons are generally used in Western cooking. Lemon peel or juice may be used as a substitute
Macadamia nuts	used as a substitute for candlenuts. Almonds can be used as a substitute for macadamia nuts
Onions	Indonesians use a small red-skinned variety. The closest substitutes are shallots but brown skinned Spanish and French onions are perfectly adequate
Palm sugar	the normal sweetening agent in Indonesian desserts. Brown sugar or molasses are good substitutes
Peanuts (kacang)	raw peanuts, dry roasted and crushed, are widely used in Indonesian cooking. An equal weight of peanut butter makes a fair substitute in some recipes
Pineapple (nenas)	indigenous to Indonesia and a favourite fruit
Pisang	see *Bananas*
Prawns, dried (ebi)	small, peeled or unpeeled prawns are sun-dried, then stored in airtight containers before use. Crushed, dried prawns can be sprinkled over a dish as a garnish. Available in Chinese grocery stores
Prawn paste (terasi, trasi, blachan)	dark brown and salty prawn or shrimp paste is sold in blocks, tins or jars. It is strong smelling and tasting and only a small amount is used to flavour a dish. Always store in an airtight container in the fridge after opening. A convenient substitute is the bottled prawn paste that can be bought in Chinese grocery stores. Anchovy flavoured soya sauce can also be used
Rambutan	a round plum-sized fruit, reddish, brownish, yellowish or greenish in colour with long hairy spines. The interior is white and fleshy with a largish stone. They are similar to lychees in taste and texture and are in season in January and from April to May

Rijst-tafel	literally means rice table. It is usually understood to mean a feast of many dishes and the phrase is used in Indonesian restaurants in Holland to describe a meal in which small amounts of a large number of different dishes are served
Sambal	a hot or spicy sauce or relish essential to an Indonesian meal. Sambals are served in a number of varieties in small bowls as accompaniments to the meal
Sambal ulek	see *Chilli peppers*
Santan	coconut milk
Sayurs	a vegetable dish cooked in coconut milk and spiced
Sereh	see *Lemon grass*
Shrimp paste	see *Prawn paste*
Soya bean curd	see *Tahu*
Soya sauce (kecap asin and kecap manis)	the English word ketchup is derived from the Indonesian/Chinese name for soya sauce, kecap. There are two varieties and they are both used in marinades, for making sauces and as a flavouring. Kecap asin is dark and salty and is available in Chinese grocery stores under the trade name Amoy (there are, however, a host of other brand names equally suitable). Avoid the light coloured, salty variety of soya sauce. It is not suitable for Indonesian cookery. Kecap manis is distinctively Indonesian and it is very thick, black and sweet. It is made from dark soya sauce and molasses. To make your own kecap manis, dissolve 2 oz (50 g) brown sugar in 6 oz (150 ml) dark soya sauce. Sprinkle it over boiled white rice. It makes boiled rice popular with children. When you are cooking with soya sauce use it sparingly, taking care not to burn the pan. Do not add extra salt until you have tasted the food
Tahu (tofu)	a soft white bean curd. It is available fresh in small square cakes from Chinese grocery stores
Tamarind (asam)	tamarind trees produce sour fruit pods which are used as a flavouring in Indonesian and Indian cookery. The pods are pressed into small balls or bricks. A portion is taken to which some water is

added. A pulp is formed which is discarded and the soaking water is used as the flavouring agent. (See page 16 for instructions on making tamarind liquid)

Tempe is a fermented soya bean product. The beans are split and parboiled and then a culture is added. The mixture is wrapped into individual portions in leaves or plastic bags and fermented for a day or two. The beans are bound together by the action of the culture and a soft white skin, similar to that on brie, forms over the surface. The finished tempe has a nutty taste and it can be cubed and added to other dishes or fried and served on its own. Tempe is sold in slabs about 1/3 in (1/4 cm) to 1 1/2 in (4 cm) thick.

Terasi, Trasi see *Prawn paste*

Turmeric spice of the same family as ginger, but without ginger's hot flavour. It is generally sold powdered and is yellow in colour. It gives curried dishes their familiar yellow-gold colour

Ulekan an Indonesian stone mortar. They cost a few pence to buy but are enormously heavy to carry home

Wok (wajan) a round-bottomed cooking utensil

INDONESIAN/ENGLISH
COOKING TERMS

asam	tamarind
agar-agar	seaweed gelatine
acar	pickles
ayam	chicken
babi	pork
babat	tripe
bawang	onion
bawang merah	red or brown onions
bawang putih	garlic
bebek	duck
beras	raw rice
blachan	prawn paste
buncis	beans
cabe	chilli
cuka	vinegar
dadar	to make omelette
daging	meat
daun	leaf
daun salem	a sort of bay leaf variety
ebi	dried prawns
gado-gado	Indonesian salad
goreng	fried
gulai	a sort of curry
gula	sugar
gula jawa	palm sugar
hati	liver
ikan	fish
jagung	sweet corn
jahe	ginger
jamur kuping	fungi
jeruk	citrus fruit
jeruk nipis	lemon
jinten	cumin

kacang	legume
kacang hijau	mung beans
kacang kapri	snow peas
kacang tanah	peanut
kal du	stock
kapulaga	cardamom
kayu manis	cinnamon
kecap	soya sauce
kecap asin	salty soya sauce
kecap manis	sweet soya sauce
kedelai	soya bean
kelapa	coconut
kemiri	candlenuts
kentang	potato
kepiting	crab
kerak	crisp fried rice or rice crust formed at bottom of rice cooking pot
ketela	sweet potato
ketumbar	coriander
ketimun	cucumber
kismis	raisins
krupuk	prawn crisps
kuah	stock
kuali	wok
kue	Indonesian cookies and cakes
kukus	steam
kunyit	turmeric
kurma	dates
lada	pepper
lengkuas	galingal root
lauk pauk	cooked dishes to be eaten with rice
lobak	turnip
lombok	chilli
manis	sweet
mentega	butter, margarine
mi	noodle
mihun	rice noodle
minyak	oil
nangka	jackfruit
nasi	cooked rice
nenas	pineapple
otak	brains
otak-otak	an Indonesian snack made of Spanish mackerel and wrapped in a banana leaf
pala	nutmeg

pepaya	papaya
petis	shrimp sauce
pecel	salad
pisang	banana
rambutan	a tropical fruit
rebung	bamboo shoot
rempeyek	fritter with batter
rujak	fruit salad
sambal	hot spicy paste or thick sauce
samin	ghee
santan	coconut milk
sate	sate (grilled pieces of meat, poultry or seafood)
sayur	vegetables
selada air	lettuce
serai	lemon grass
sop	soup
soun	transparent noodles
tahu	bean curd
tape	fermented sweet glutinous rices
tauco	fermented brown beans
tauge	beansprouts
telur	egg
telur dadar	omelette
tempe	soya bean cake
tepung beras	rice flour
tepung gandum	wheat flour
tepung jagung	cornflour
tepung ketan	glutinous rice flour
terasi	prawn paste
terung	eggplant
tiram	oyster
tomat	tomato
tumis	sauté
ubi	sweet potato
udang	prawns
udang kering	dried prawns
vetsin	MSG (monosodium glutamate)
wajan	wok
wijen	sesame seeds
wortel	carrot

SOUPS
(Sop and Soto)

In Indonesia, soups are not invariably served at the beginning of a meal but very often as part of it. They are normally substantial and contain a number of ingredients. Soup either accompanies rice or noodles or has them in it. In Indonesia there are two words for soup, soto, which is a soup, eaten on its own as an all-purpose, filling dish at social gatherings or as a light meal in itself, and sop a thin, lighter soup. For the purposes of this book, I have called the thick soups soto and the thin soups sop. If you enjoy spicy, filling soups you will like the Indonesian variety.

A great surprise to me when I visited Indonesia was the discovery that oxtail soup was very popular. It must have been introduced by the Dutch, but it has been enthusiastically adopted and improved by the Indonesians. A strange sight to come across in the market place is a line of oxtails each supported over a burning candle. My first thought on seeing this was that it was either a novel slow cooking method or a bizarre religious rite. The answer is more mundane: it's just a good way of keeping the flies away.

Spiced Chicken Soup (Soto Ayam)

Soto ayam is a popular soup and there are many variations. I have given two here. In the first recipe the soup is served in the normal way and then garnished. In the second the stock and cooked ingredients are separated and each person makes up his or her own soup bowl by individually selecting a combination of the cooked ingredients and additional accompaniments, over which the separated stock is then poured.

Method 1
Serves 6–8

In this method the soup is served in the normal manner and then garnished.

2 tablespoons vegetable oil
1 medium onion, finely chopped
3 cloves garlic, crushed
1/2-in (1-cm) piece root ginger, finely chopped
1 teaspoon coriander seeds, crushed
1/2 teaspoon cayenne pepper
1 tablespoon crushed macadamia nuts *or* crunchy peanut butter
2 lb (1 kg) chicken, quartered *or* chicken pieces
3 pints (1.7 litres) water
salt and pepper to taste

To garnish

lemon or lime wedges plus one or two of the following:
1–2 sticks young celery, finely chopped
2 hard-boiled eggs, sliced
4 spring onions, chopped
4 oz (100 g) cooked noodles
4 oz (100 g) cooked rice
2 medium carrots, peeled and grated

Heat the oil in a heavy saucepan and add the onion, garlic and ginger. Stir over a low heat until the onion is softened. Add the coriander, cayenne and the macadamia nuts or peanut butter and stir for 2–3 minutes. Put in the chicken pieces, move them around the pan and coat both sides of each piece with the spice mixture. Cook for a further 2 minutes, turning the chicken over once during this time. Pour in the water and season to taste with salt and pepper. Bring to the boil, reduce the heat, cover and simmer for 45 minutes or until the chicken is tender. Remove the chicken and leave the stock to simmer, uncovered for 15 minutes. Take the chicken meat and skin off the bones and cut it into small pieces. Distribute the chicken pieces around the soup bowls and add a selection of the garnishings. Adjust the seasoning of the stock and then pour it into the bowls. Garnish each bowl and serve with lemon wedges, letting each diner squeeze in lemon juice to taste.

Variation: Ten minutes before the end of the cooking time add 4 oz (100 g) of fresh peeled prawns to the boiling chicken and serve them with the chicken pieces.

Method 2
Serves 6–8

In this method the chicken, once cooked, is removed from the stock and served separately along with other cooked accompaniments.

2 lb (1 kg) chicken, quartered *or*
  chicken pieces
salt and pepper to taste
2 tablespoons vegetable oil
1 medium onion, finely diced
2 cloves garlic, crushed
1/2-in (1-cm) piece root ginger,
  finely chopped
1 teaspoon ground turmeric
1/2 teaspoon chilli powder
1 teaspoon grated lemon rind
  or chopped lemon grass
6 oz (175 g) beansprouts

6 oz (175 g) cabbage, shredded
4 oz (100 g) cooked noodles
4 oz (100 g) cooked rice
2 hard-boiled eggs, shelled and
  sliced (optional)

To garnish

1–2 sticks young celery, finely
  chopped
3–4 spring onions or shallots,
  finely chopped
lemon or lime wedges

Put the chicken in a large saucepan and cover with water. Season to taste with salt and pepper and bring to the boil. Cover, reduce the heat and set to simmer. Heat the oil in a small frying pan and add the onion, garlic and ginger. Fry stirring until the onion is softened. Add the turmeric, chili powder and lemon rind or lemon grass and continue frying and stirring for another minute. Put this spice mixture into the pot with the simmering chicken. Cover the pot and leave to simmer for 40 minutes or until the chicken is tender. Remove the chicken from the pot and leave the stock on a low simmer. Take the chicken meat and skin off the bone, slice it thinly and arrange the slices on a serving plate. Separately, scald the beansprouts and shredded cabbage briefly in boiling water. Drain and arrange on serving dishes. Transfer the cooked noodles and rice to a separate serving bowl. Adjust the seasoning of the stock to taste and pour it into a large soup bowl. To serve, put the soup bowl in the centre of the table and surround it with cooked rice, eggs, chicken, beansprouts, cabbage and noodles and garnishings. Each person puts a mixture of cooked ingredients into his or her bowl, pours over soup stock and garnishes it with celery, shallots and lemon juice.

Curried Chicken Soup
(Soto Ayam Bumbu Kari)

Serves 6

2 lb (1 kg) chicken, quartered *or* chicken pieces
2 curry leaves (optional)
2 tablespoons vegetable oil
1 medium onion, diced
2 cloves garlic, crushed
1 tablespoon crushed macadamia nuts *or* crunchy peanut butter
1 teaspoon curry powder
1/2 teaspoon chilli powder
1/2 teaspoon ground ginger
3 oz (75 g) Chinese noodles covered in hot water for 5 minutes, rinsed in cold water and drained
juice of 1 lemon
salt to taste

Put the chicken and curry leaves (if used) into a heavy saucepan, cover with 2 pints (1 litre) of water, bring to the boil, reduce heat, cover and simmer for 45 minutes or until the chicken is tender. Meanwhile, put the oil in a frying pan and lightly fry the onion and garlic. Stir in the curry powder, macadamia nuts, chilli powder and ginger and lightly cook for 2 minutes. Remove the cooked chicken from the stock and cut the meat and skin away from the bones. Leave the stock on a low simmer. Chop the meat and skin into small pieces and add it to the frying pan. Coat the meat in the spice mixture and transfer the contents of the pan to the stock. Bring the soup to the boil, add the noodles, adjust the seasoning, add the lemon juice, stir well and serve. Cooked rice may also replace the noodles.

Meatballs with Vegetable Soup (Sop Bakso)

Serves 6

The meatballs made for this soup go well with other soups and the vegetable soup to which they are added is also good on its own or as a base for noodle soup.

Meatballs

8 oz (225 g) finely minced lean beef (double minced if necessary)
1 small onion, finely diced
1/2 teaspoon salt
1/4 teaspoon white pepper
1 tablespoon cornflour
1 egg white

Vegetable soup

2 tablespoons vegetable oil
1 medium onion, finely sliced
2 cloves garlic, crushed
1/2 teaspoon finely grated root
    ginger *or* ground ginger
1 tablespoon dark soya sauce
2 1/2 pints (1.5 litres) vegetable or
    chicken stock

2 medium carrots, peeled and
    sliced
4 oz (100 g) cabbage leaves,
    chopped *or* 4 Chinese cabbage
    leaves, cut in half
salt and pepper to taste

To garnish

1 small onion *or* 2 shallots, diced
    and browned in a little oil

Combine the minced meat, onion, pepper and salt in a bowl and mix them together, thoroughly. Add the cornflour and egg white, knead the mixture well and shape it into meatballs 1 in (2 cm) in diameter. Set them aside. To make the soup. Heat the oil in a heavy pan and add the onion and garlic. Sauté them over a low heat until the onion is softened. Stir in the ginger, soya sauce, stock, carrots and cabbage leaves. Bring to the boil, reduce the heat and simmer until the carrots are almost tender (about 10 minutes). Lower the meatballs into the soup a few at a time, until they are all added. Return the soup to the boil, reduce the heat and simmer for 5–7 minutes or until the meatballs are cooked. Season to taste with salt and pepper and serve garnished with fried onion or shallot.

Variation: Instead of cabbage you can use 6 oz (175 g) of chopped spinach, sautéed in a little oil before it is added to the soup.

Meatball Soup with Noodles (Mi Bakso)

Serves 6

4 oz (100 g) noodles

Prepare the meatballs with vegetable soup as above. Cook the noodles in a pan of boiling salted water, until just tender. Drain, rinse them under cold water and set aside. Add these noodles to the cooked soup, heat through and serve.

Spicy Oxtail Soup (Sop Buntut)

Serves 6

2 oz (50 g) cornflour
½ teaspoon ground cumin
1 teaspoon ground coriander
½ teaspoon ground turmeric
½ teaspoon chilli powder
1 medium oxtail cut into sections
3 tablespoons vegetable oil *or* 2 oz (50 g) butter

3 cloves garlic, crushed
2 medium onions, sliced
2 medium carrots, thinly sliced
2½ pints (1.5 litres) water *or* stock
salt and pepper to taste
2 tablespoons dark soya sauce
2 teaspoons brown sugar

Combine the cornflour, cumin, coriander, turmeric and chilli powder, mix them well together and roll the oxtail pieces in the mixture. Heat the oil or butter in a heavy saucepan and lightly brown the oxtail pieces all over. Add the garlic and onions and stir and cook over a low heat until the onions are softened. Add the carrots and water or stock and season to taste with salt and pepper. Bring the soup to the boil, reduce heat, cover and simmer for about 2 hours or until the oxtail is very tender. Adjust the seasoning, stir in the soya sauce and sugar and serve.

Prawn Soup (Soto Udang)

Serves 4

This soup is best if made with fresh prawns although frozen prawns can be used if you have a good stock available. To prepare fresh prawns for the soup, remove the head, tail, legs and shell and, if the prawns are large, remove the vein along the back with a sharp knife. This soup can also be made with coconut milk. See variation below.

2 tablespoons vegetable oil
2 cloves garlic, crushed
½-in (1-cm) piece root ginger, finely chopped
2 small onions, finely sliced
1 teaspoon ground coriander

6 oz (175 g) fresh *or* frozen prawns, peeled and cleaned
1½ pints (850 ml) water *or* stock
salt and pepper to taste
4 oz (100 g) noodles
1 small leek, thinly sliced

Heat the oil in a heavy pan, add the garlic, ginger and onions and sauté, stirring until the onion is softened. Add the coriander powder and prawns and cook, stirring, for 2–3 minutes. Pour in the water or stock and season to taste with salt and pepper. Bring to the boil, reduce heat and simmer for 15 minutes. Add the noodles, stir well and simmer for a further 10 minutes. Add the leek, adjust the seasoning and cook the soup gently for another 5 minutes. Serve.

Variation: Substitute fresh or canned coconut milk (for preparation from desiccated coconut see page 15) for half the stock or water. Follow the same procedure as given in the recipe but after adding the water or stock and coconut milk mixture to the prawns, stir the soup continuously until it comes to the boil and then only allow it to simmer very gently. The stirring and gentle simmering prevent the coconut milk from curdling.

Fish Soup (Soto Ikan)

Serves 6–8

2 lb (1 kg) white fish, filleted, reserve skin, head and bones
2½ pints (1.5 litres) water
1 lb (450 g) tomatoes
1 teaspoon grated lemon rind *or* freshly chopped lemon grass
1 medium onion, diced

2 cloves garlic
½-in (1-cm) piece root ginger, chopped
1 tablespoon lemon juice *or* tamarind water
salt and pepper to taste

Put the reserved skin, bones and head of the filleted fish (but not the fish) into a pan with the water. Bring to the boil, reduce the heat, cover and simmer for 1 hour. Drain, discard the bones and reserve the stock. Scald the tomatoes briefly in boiling water, skin and chop them. Put the stock back in the pan, add the tomatoes and lemon rind or lemon grass and bring to the boil. Reduce the heat and leave to simmer. Put the onion, garlic, ginger and a tablespoon of the fish stock into a blender or food processor and blend them to a paste. Alternatively, dice the onion, garlic and ginger very small and crush them with a pestle and mortar to a paste. Add the paste to the stock, stir well and simmer for 5 minutes. Cut the filleted fish into pieces, add to the stock and simmer for 20 minutes. Stir in the lemon juice or tamarind water, season to taste and serve.

Javanese Vegetable Soup (Sayur Lodeh)

Serves 6

This is a delicious spicy soup made thick and creamy by the addition of coconut milk. Use a combination of vegetables to your liking, adding them to the pot in the order in which they cook, that is to say, the one that cooks longest the first. If you reduce the quantity of water given in the recipe by half, the soup becomes a vegetable main dish suitable for serving with rice.

Select 1 lb (450 g) of one or a variety of vegetables. The following are suggestions: white cabbage, shredded; cauliflower, cut into florets; aubergines, sliced, salted and left for 30 minutes, rinsed and drained. French beans, topped, tailed and cut into 2½-in (5-cm) lengths; Chinese cabbage, coarsely chopped; watercress; spinach, chopped; courgettes, thinly sliced; carrots, thinly sliced. You will also need the following:

2 pints (1 litre) water
1 medium onion, finely diced
2 cloves garlic, crushed
½–1 green or red chilli, finely chopped
2 bay leaves or daun salem leaves
1 teaspoon grated lemon rind or chopped lemon grass

1½ teaspoons ground coriander
1 teaspoon dark brown sugar
1 teaspoon prawn paste (optional)
8 fl oz (225 ml) coconut milk (see page 14)
salt and pepper to taste

Prepare the vegetables. Bring the water to the boil in a heavy saucepan. Add the onion, garlic and chilli, bay leaves, lemon rind or lemon grass, coriander, brown sugar and prawn paste, if used. Stir well, cover and leave to simmer for 15 minutes. Now add the vegetables in order of their cooking times, leaving the quick-cooking, leafy ones like watercress or spinach to the very end. After all the vegetables have been added, continue cooking until they are very tender. Stir in the coconut milk, season to taste with salt and pepper and return the soup to a gentle boil, stirring constantly. Simmer for 5 minutes and then serve.

Spinach (or Watercress) and Ginger Soup (Sop Bayam Jahe)

Serves 4

This soup is normally served with the addition of diced cooked pork or chicken. I have included them in the ingredients but the flavour of the soup is unaffected if you leave them out.

2 tablespoons vegetable oil
1-in (2.5-cm) piece root ginger, finely chopped
1 oz (25 g) raw peanuts, dry roasted and crushed or 1½ teaspoons crunchy peanut butter
1½ pints (850 ml) water or stock, boiling

10 oz (275 g) watercress or fresh spinach, finely chopped
4 oz (100 g) cooked lean pork or cooked chicken, diced (optional)
1 teaspoon cornflour
½ teaspoon ground turmeric
1 tablespoon dark soya sauce
½ teaspoon dark brown sugar
salt and pepper to taste

Heat the oil in a saucepan, add the ginger and stir fry it gently for 2 minutes. Add the crushed peanuts or peanut butter and stir fry for 1 minute. Pour in the boiling water or stock, add the watercress or spinach and set the pan to simmer, covered, for 5 minutes. Combine in a small bowl the pork or chicken (if used), cornflour, turmeric, soya sauce, sugar, salt and pepper to taste and 2 tablespoons of stock from the soup. Make the mixture into a paste and stir this into the soup, leaving it to simmer, covered, for a further 10 minutes. Adjust the seasoning and serve.

Variation: To pep up the soup, add 1 or 2 finely chopped chilli peppers when you cook the ginger.

Bamboo Shoots and Cabbage Soup (Sop Kol Rebung)

Serves 6

This soup is served with boiled rice. Some of the soup stock is used to moisten the rice, the soup vegetables are then spooned over it and the stock is served in a separate bowl. Vegetables other than cabbage can be used. See variations below.

2 pints (1 litre) vegetable stock
1 medium onion, finely diced
2 cloves garlic, crushed
1-in (2.5-cm) piece root ginger, finely chopped
1 teaspoon prawn paste (optional)
1 lb (450 g) tomatoes
2 bay leaves *or* daun salem leaves

1 lb (450 g) cabbage leaves, chopped
4 oz (100 g) tinned bamboo shoots, sliced
1 tablespoon lemon juice *or* tamarind water
salt and pepper to taste

Heat the stock in a pan and add the onion, garlic, ginger and prawn paste, if used. Bring to the boil, cover and set to simmer. Scald the tomatoes briefly in boiling water, remove the skins and chop them into quarters. Put the tomatoes into the stock pan, add the bay leaves or daun salem leaves, stir well and season to taste with salt and pepper. Leave the soup to simmer for another 15 minutes. Add the cabbage and bamboo shoots, stir well and return the pan to the boil. Reduce the heat to low and simmer, covered, for 30 minutes or until the cabbage is very tender. Stir in the lemon juice or tamarind water, adjust the seasoning and serve with boiled rice.

Variations: You can substitute carrots, potatoes, courgettes, aubergines or French beans for the cabbage leaves and proceed as directed in the recipe.

Spicy Beef Soup (Soto Daging)

Serves 6–8

1 lb (450 g) brisket of beef, boned
   and tied into a roll with string
salt and pepper to taste
2½ pints (1.5 litres) water
2 tablespoons oil
2 small onions, finely diced
4 cloves garlic, crushed
1-in (2.5-cm) piece root ginger,
   finely chopped

½ teaspoon ground turmeric
4 macadamia nuts *or* almonds,
   crushed
1 chilli, finely chopped (optional)

To garnish
½ small onion, sliced and browned
   in a little oil
lemon or lime wedges

Put the piece of beef into a pan, add salt and pepper to taste, add the water and bring to the boil. Reduce the heat, cover the pan and leave to simmer until the meat is almost tender (about 1½ hours). Remove the meat from the pan and set it aside. Leave the stock in the pan. In a small frying pan, heat the oil, add the onions, garlic and ginger and stir fry them until the onions are soft. Add the turmeric, crushed nuts and chilli and stir the mixture over a moderate heat for 2–3 minutes. Add this mixture to the stock in the pan and stir well. Slice the meat and cut it into about 2-in (5-cm) squares. Return the meat slices to the pan. Cover the soup and leave it to simmer over a low heat until the meat is tender. Season to taste with salt and pepper and serve garnished with the fried onions. Serve the lemon or lime wedges in a separate bowl.

Chinese Cabbage and Pork Soup (Sop Sawi Dengan Babi)

Serves 4

This is a quick soup to prepare and the flavour and method illustrate its Chinese origins.

1 teaspoon cornflour
1 tablespoon dark soya sauce
2 teaspoons dark brown sugar
2 cloves garlic, crushed
4 oz (100 g) lean pork, sliced
   thinly

1½ pints (850 ml) vegetable,
   chicken *or* other stock (bouillon
   cubes could be used)
1 small head Chinese cabbage,
   chopped
salt and black pepper to taste

Put the cornflour, soya sauce, sugar and garlic into a bowl and stir the mixture into a paste, adding a little stock if necessary. Stir the pork slices into the paste, coating each piece. Bring the stock to the boil in a saucepan, add the cabbage leaves and cook them, stirring, over a moderate heat until they have wilted. Stir in the pork pieces and season the soup to taste with salt and black pepper. Cover, reduce the heat and simmer for 10 minutes. Serve.

Prawn and Courgette Soup (Sop Udang)

Serves 4–6

This spicy soup is designed to be served with rice and a main dish, such as curry. The rice is moistened with stock from the soup before it is eaten.

2 tablespoons vegetable oil
1 medium onion, finely sliced
2 cloves garlic, crushed
2 fresh *or* dried red chillies, seeded and finely chopped
6 oz (175 g) fresh prawns, shelled and cleaned *or* tinned *or* frozen prawns (defrosted), chopped

8 oz (225 g) courgettes, sliced
1 tablespoon tomato purée
2 bay leaves *or* daun salem leaves
16 fl oz (450 ml) vegetable *or* chicken stock
8 fl oz (225 ml) coconut milk
salt and pepper to taste

Heat the oil in a heavy saucepan and sauté the onion, garlic and chillies until the onion is golden in colour. Add the prawns and courgettes and continue cooking and stirring over a moderate heat for 3–4 minutes. Add the tomato purée, bay leaves or daun salem leaves and stock and mix well. Cover the pan and simmer for 15 minutes. Stir in the coconut milk, add salt and pepper to taste and simmer for a further 5 minutes, stirring. Serve.

RELISHES,
SAUCES AND GARNISHES
(Sambal and Saos)

RELISHES AND SAUCES (Sambal and Saos)

Sambals are hot and/or spicy sauces or relishes which are served as
accompaniments to other dishes and they form a very important part
of an Indonesian meal. Chilli peppers are the most common ingredient
and, consequently, sambals are often very hot, even fiery. They are
served in very small bowls and you season your own food with the
right amount for your taste. People unused to very hot food are
advised to start by adding only the smallest amount of particularly hot
sambals to their food. Indonesian chefs take into account that sambals
will accompany the dishes they serve and thus will be more likely to
under- rather than over-season a dish. It's very much a question of
personal choice about which sambals to serve with which dishes, but if
you remember that sambals are chosen and added to enhance the
dishes and not to overpower them, you won't go far wrong. Sambals
can also be added in very small amounts to soups, sauces and dressings
if they need a little extra bite.

The ingredients for making a sambal are usually crushed together into a paste with a stone pestle and mortar (ulek-ulek and cobek). If you do not have them a blender or food grinder will do the job as well (see page 17). Where appropriate in the recipes I have given, I have suggested using a food blender (the quantities concerned are small so a blender with a small container or an electric grinder are most suitable) but you may in each case use a pestle and mortar if you wish.

Where fresh or dried chillies are unavailable, substitute 1 teaspoon of chilli powder or sauce for 2 fresh or dried chilli peppers. Where prawn or shrimp paste is recommended but unavailable, you may substitute 1 anchovy fillet for each teaspoon of paste.

Most sambals keep well and are useful to have around. They should be kept in sterilized, airtight containers and refrigerated. The amounts I have given in some of the recipes will normally make enough for 2 or 3 meals, depending of course on how much sambal is needed (this is determined by how hot it is) and on how many people you are serving. These are marked as serving 8–10. Where the recipe only makes enough for one meal they are marked as serving 4.

Chilli Paste (Sambal Ulek)

Serves 8–10

This is the most basic sambal and is made by seeding and chopping many chilli peppers, grinding them into a paste and boiling the paste with a little water and salt. The sambal is bottled and used as required. Hot chilli sauce (the Chinese variety), although smoother than genuine sambal ulek, is a good substitute. Sambal ulek is also available commercially in Australia and Holland. Here is a variation on the basic sambal ulek recipe that is worth making at home.

8–10 fresh *or* dried red chillies
1 small onion, diced
2 cloves garlic
1 teaspoon brown sugar
2 tablespoons water

1 teaspoon grated lemon peel *or* chopped lemon grass
1/2 teaspoon salt
2 tablespoons vegetable oil

Put all the ingredients except the oil into a blender and process the mixture to a smooth paste or use a pestle and mortar. Heat the oil in a small pan or wok and stir in the paste. Cook over a low heat for 7–8 minutes, stirring. It is now ready to serve. Store unused paste in a clean, airtight jar in the refrigerator. It will keep for many weeks.

Variation: Add 1 oz (25 g) roasted peanuts to the ingredients. This gives a thick, slightly milder sambal.

Vinegar and Chilli Sauce (Sambal Cuka)

Serves 8–10

This hot, sour sambal is good as a contrast to sweet or mild flavoured dishes.

8–10 fresh *or* dried chillies
1/2-in (1-cm) piece of root ginger,
   peeled *or* 1/2 teaspoon ground
   ginger

2 cloves garlic
3 tablespoons white vinegar
1 tablespoon brown sugar
1 teaspoon salt

Put all the ingredients into a blender and process the mixture to a smooth paste. It is now ready to serve. Store unused paste in a clean, airtight jar in the refrigerator. It will keep for several weeks.

Fresh Tomato and Chilli Sauce (Sambal Tomat)

Serves 8–10

This is a quick sauce to make and it does not require any cooking. It is good with cold or uncooked dishes. The fried version, recipe below, is better with hot dishes and also keeps longer.

1 lb (450 g) ripe tomatoes
2 or 3 fresh *or* dried red chillies
2 tablespoons water
2 cloves garlic
1/2-in (1-cm) piece root ginger,
   peeled *or* 1/2 teaspoon ground
   ginger

1 tablespoon brown sugar
2 teaspoons salt
2 teaspoons prawn paste (optional)
2 teaspoons lemon juice

Scald the tomatoes in boiling water and peel off the skins. Put the remaining ingredients into a blender and process the mixture to a paste. Add the tomatoes and switch on the machine briefly to combine the paste and tomatoes. Serve immediately or store in a sterilized jar for use as required. It will keep for 2 or 3 weeks in a refrigerator.

Fried Tomato and Chilli Sauce (Sambal Tomat Tumis)

Serves 8–10

The ingredients are the same as for fresh tomato and chilli sauce with the addition of 4 fl oz (100 ml) of vegetable oil. Prepare the tomato sauce as above. Heat the oil in a small pan or wok and stir in the sauce.

Stir and cook it over a moderate heat for 7–8 minutes. Add more water if the paste gets too thick. Serve immediately. Store unused sauce in an airtight jar. It will keep for several weeks in a refrigerator.

Chilli Hot Peanut Sauce (Sambal Kacang)

Serves 4

This is a tasty but not too hot sambal. It also provides the basis for making other sambals. See variations below.

4 oz (100 g) roasted, unsalted peanuts
2 red chillies
2 cloves garlic

2 tablespoons dark soya sauce
2 tablespoons white vinegar
2 teaspoons brown sugar

Put all the ingredients into a blender and blend until smooth. If the mixture is too thick add water, a tablespoon at a time, until the consistency is that of very thick mustard. Store unused sambal in an airtight jar in the refrigerator. It will keep for several weeks.

Variations

1. Add 8 oz (225 g) scalded and peeled tomatoes to the ingredients and blend as above. Add salt if required.
2. Add 4 fl oz (100 ml) fresh or canned coconut milk (see page 14) to the mixture during blending. Add salt as required. Store in an airtight jar in the refrigerator.
3. Leave out the salt and add 1 teaspoon of prawn paste or 2 anchovy fillets during blending. Add salt at the end if necessary.

Quick Garlic and Chilli Sauce (Sambal Jelantah)

Serves 4

2 tablespoons vegetable oil
4 cloves garlic, crushed
2 fresh *or* dried red chillies, finely chopped

1/2 small onion, finely diced
1 teaspoon prawn paste (optional)
salt to taste

Heat the oil in a small pan or wok, add the garlic, chillies and onion and cook, stirring, for 2–3 minutes. Add the prawn paste, if used, and salt to taste. Stir and heat for another minute. Serve hot or cold.

Coconut sauce (Sambal Kelapa)

Coconut sauce is made in cooked and uncooked varieties. The uncooked should be used when it is made, the cooked will keep for up to a week in an airtight jar in a refrigerator. Both coconut sambals can either be served in a side bowl or sprinkled directly over the dish which is to be seasoned. They are good with main meals, soups, rice and salads.

Uncooked Coconut Sauce

Serves 4

4 oz (100 g) desiccated coconut
2 tablespoons water
2 fresh *or* dried red chillies, finely
   chopped

1 teaspoon grated lemon peel *or*
   chopped lemon grass
1 tablespoon diced onion
1 clove garlic, finely chopped
salt to taste

Sprinkle the water over the coconut in a bowl and mix well. Add all the other ingredients and stir well.

Cooked Coconut Sauce

Serves 4

2 tablespoons vegetable oil
2 fresh *or* dried red chillies
1 small onion, finely diced
1/4 teaspoon prawn paste (optional)

4 oz (100 g) desiccated coconut
1 teaspoon grated lemon peel *or*
   chopped lemon grass
salt to taste

Heat the oil in a small pan or wok and add the chillies and onion. Stir fry until softened. Stir in the prawn paste, if used, the coconut and lemon peel or lemon grass. Stir and cook over a low heat until the coconut is lightly browned. Season with salt and serve. Or store in an airtight jar in the refrigerator.

Spiced Chilli Sauce (Sambal Bajak)

Serves 8–10

This is a popular sambal made in many variations (see below). It will keep for weeks in an airtight jar in a refrigerator. If you wish to make only enough for one meal, quarter the amounts given here.

10 fresh *or* dried red chillies

2 small onions *or* 4 shallots, finely
diced

1/2 teaspoon prawn paste *or* 1
tablespoon chopped fresh
shrimps or prawns, *or* tinned
anchovy

3 tablespoons water

1 teaspoon dark brown sugar

2 cloves garlic

4 macadamia nuts *or* almonds

1/2 teaspoon finely grated root
ginger *or* ground ginger

2 tablespoons white vinegar

2 fl oz (50 ml) vegetable oil

Put all the ingredients, except the oil, into a blender and process into a
smooth paste. Heat the oil in a small pan or wok and stir in the paste.
Stir and cook it over a low heat for 5 minutes. Serve or store.

Spiced Chilli Sauce with Coconut Milk
Serves 8–10

After preparing the sambal as above, leave it in the pan and add 6 fl oz
(175 ml) fresh or canned coconut milk (see page 14). Stir well and cook
gently over a very low heat, uncovered, for a further 15 minutes. Do
not allow it to boil. Serve or use within 2 days of preparation.

Spiced Chilli Sauce with Tomatoes
Serves 8–10

Add 1 lb (450 g) ripe tomatoes, scalded with boiling water and peeled,
to the ingredients in the basic recipe and proceed as directed.

Soya and Chilli Sauce (Sambal Kecap)

Serves 4

This is simple and quick to make and is a suitable accompaniment to
most dishes. To make enough for storage, double the amounts given
and store unused sambal in an airtight jar in the refrigerator. It will
keep for several weeks. There are two methods of preparation. Sauce 1
is sweeter than Sauce 2.

Sauce 1

2 fl oz (50 ml) dark soya sauce

1 or 2 fresh *or* dried red chillies,
finely chopped

1 clove garlic, finely chopped

1 tablespoon dark brown sugar *or*
molasses

Sauce 2

2 fl oz (50 ml) dark soya sauce

1 or 2 fresh *or* dried red chillies,
finely chopped

1 small onion *or* 2 shallots, finely
diced

juice of 1 lemon *or* lime

1 clove garlic, crushed

For both the sauces, combine the ingredients in a small pan and mix well. Cook, stirring, over a low heat for 5 minutes.

Variation: Add 1 or 2 teaspoons of toasted sesame seeds to the sambal.

Cucumber Pickle (Acar Ketimun)

Serves 4

1 medium cucumber, peeled
1 tablespoon salt
4 fl oz (100 ml) white vinegar
1½ tablespoons white sugar

1 red chilli, fresh *or* dried, finely chopped
salt to taste

Slice the cucumber down the middle lengthwise and remove the seeds, dice very finely and put the pieces in a sieve or colander. Sprinkle salt over them, shake and leave for 20 minutes. Rinse them with water and drain for 20 minutes. Gently heat the vinegar and dissolve the sugar in it. Combine the cucumber, vinegar and sugar solution and chilli in a bowl. Salt the mixture to taste and set it aside to cool before serving.

Vic's Viking Cucumber Pickle (Acar Ketimun Vic's Viking)

Serves 8–10

The recipes for this pickle and the mixed pickle that follows are from the famous Vic's Viking restaurant in Jakarta where they serve a huge and delicious array of dishes in a help-yourself buffet. The cucumber pickle is particularly good with fried rice or fried chicken and it is also very soothing to the tongue after a dish hot with chillies.

2 lb (1 kg) small pickling
 cucumbers
2 fresh large red chillies, seeded
2 fl oz (50 ml) white vinegar

4 fl oz (100 ml) water
1 lb (450 g) white sugar
1 teaspoon salt

Blanch the cucumbers and chillies in boiling water for a few seconds, remove them and drain. Cut the cucumbers crosswise into ½-in (1-cm) thick slices. Cut the chillies once lengthwise and then thinly slice them crosswise. Combine all the ingredients in a bowl and leave them, uncovered, for 3 to 5 hours. Stir occasionally. Initially there will not be enough liquid to cover the cucumbers but slowly liquid from the cucumbers will seep out. Store unused pickle in clean airtight glass jars in the refrigerator.

Vic's Viking Mustard Mixed Pickle (Acar Moster Vic's Viking)

Serves 8–10

8 oz (225 g) small pickling
  cucumbers, cut into ½-in (1-cm)
  thick slices
8 oz (225 g) shallots, peeled, cut
  into halves
8 oz (225 g) carrots, peeled, cut
  lengthwise into matchsticks

8 oz (225 g) cauliflower florets
2 fl oz (50 ml) white vinegar
4 fl oz (100 ml) water
1 lb (450 g) white sugar
1 tablespoon mustard powder
1 teaspoon salt

Blanch the cucumbers, shallots, carrots and cauliflower in boiling water for a few seconds, remove them and drain. Combine all the ingredients in a bowl and leave uncovered for 3 to 5 hours. Stir occasionally. Store unused pickle in clean airtight glass jars in the refrigerator.

Peanut Sauce (Saos Kacang)

Serves 4

This is a relatively mild sauce which is very good poured over cooked vegetables. For a quick version using peanut butter, see quick peanut sauce recipe (page 50).

8 oz (225 g) raw unsalted peanuts
2 tablespoons vegetable oil
2 fresh *or* dried red chillies, finely
  chopped (for a hot sauce,
  otherwise leave them out)
1 small onion, diced
2 cloves garlic, crushed

juice of 1 lemon *or* lime
4 fl oz (100 ml) water
1 tablespoon dark soya sauce
1 tablespoon vegetable oil
salt to taste
water *or* coconut milk for thinning

Combine the peanuts and oil in a bowl, mix well. Spread the peanuts on a flat tray and place the tray in a moderate oven 350° F (180° C, gas mark 4) for 5–8 minutes or until the peanuts are roasted light brown. Put the roasted peanuts together with all the other ingredients into a blender and process the mixture to a thick paste. Transfer the paste to a pan and stir, cooking it over a low heat for 5 minutes. Thin the sauce to the thickness you require by adding water or coconut milk while continuing to stir over a low heat. Alternatively, store the undiluted sauce in a jar and thin as required or use it very thick as a relish or spread.

Quick Peanut Sauce

Serves 4

The preparation of this sauce is speeded up by making use of peanut butter as the base ingredient. It's mild in flavour but it can be pepped up by adding 1 teaspoon of chilli sauce or powder to the finished sauce.

3 oz (75 g) crunchy peanut butter
8 fl oz (225 ml) hot water *or* fresh
　or canned coconut milk
1 clove garlic, crushed

2 tablespoons dark soya sauce
juice of 1 lemon *or* lime
2 teaspoons dark brown sugar
salt to taste

Put all the ingredients into a blender and process the mixture to a smooth paste. Alternatively, stir the peanut butter in the hot water, or coconut milk, over a low heat until mixed and then stir in the remaining ingredients. Finally, if needed, thin the sauce by adding a little more water or coconut milk.

GARNISHES

Indonesian dishes are often garnished before being served. The cook will use chopped herbs, chopped nuts, finely sliced chilli peppers or anything colourful and suitable which is to hand. Below are details of some popular cooked garnishes.

Fried Onion Flakes (Bawang Goreng)

Fried onion flakes are used as an all-round garnish although they are particularly good with soups. They are most easily made from dried onion rings, but taste best made from fresh onions.

From dried (dehydrated) onion rings
Serves 4 as a garnish

4 oz (100 g) dried onion rings
4 fl oz (100 ml) vegetable oil

Heat the oil in a heavy 8-in (20-cm) frying pan. Stir in the onion rings and cook, stirring, until nicely browned. Drain the onions through a sieve and then pat them gently between absorbent sheets of kitchen paper. They are now ready for use. Store unused onion flakes in an airtight jar. They will keep well for up to a week.

From fresh onions
Serves 4 as a garnish

2 medium onions, finely sliced
4 fl oz (100 ml) vegetable oil

Press the onion rings between sheets of absorbent kitchen paper to remove the moisture and then follow the same method as for the dried onion rings.

Prawn Crackers (Krupuk Udang)

Prawn crackers, as their name implies, are made from a batter flavoured with prawns. They are nearly always bought dried and ready for deep frying. The Indonesian variety called krupuk are about 4 in (10 cm) long and they puff up to 2 or 3 times that size when deep fried. Krupuk are eaten with almost any savoury meal and can also be broken into pieces and used to garnish a dish. To cook crackers heat about 10 fl oz (275 ml) of oil in an 8-in (20-cm) deep frying pan or wok. Drop a single cracker in and keep it pressed flat for the first few seconds with the back of a fish slice. It will swell in size almost immediately and is then drained and removed from the pan. Repeat for as many crackers as you need. To taste them at their best, use them right away. However, you can store them in an airtight container and they will stay moderately crisp for 2 to 3 days.

Potato Crisps (Kripik Kentang)

Potato crisps made at home are used in Indonesia as a garnish for salad and vegetable dishes. Our own bags of crisps can be substituted.

Egg Garnishings (Hiasan Telur)

Quartered or sliced hard-boiled eggs or slices of thin omelette are used as a garnish for meat, vegetable and rice dishes.

Marbled Eggs (Telur Berwarna)

Festive meals are often garnished with halved hard-boiled eggs that have been marbled with different colours. The process is quite simple and relies upon food colouring.

Put the required number of eggs in a pan and cover them with salted cold water. Bring them to a gentle boil while stirring. Leave on a low boil for another 8 minutes and then drain the eggs and cool them under running water. Put 2 or 3 different concentrated solutions of food colouring (perhaps red, yellow or green) and water into 2 or 3 pans and bring them to the boil. Gently crack the shells of the hard-boiled eggs all over. Divide the eggs between the pans and simmer them in the coloured water for 5 minutes. Remove the pans from the heat and leave the eggs in them for 1 hour. Remove the eggs from the pans and shell them. The whites will be brightly mottled with whichever colour dye was used.

Egg Yolk Centring Technique

It is more pleasing to the eye if, when garnishing with boiled egg slices, the yolk is in the centre. This is achieved quite simply by turning the eggs around with a spoon, every minute or so while they are hard boiling.

SAVOURY
SNACKS AND SWEETS
(Makanan Kecil and Cuci Mulut)

One of the delights of Indonesia is the variety of its street life which day and night is a carnival of people selling their wares. The most popular hawkers are those pushing colourful movable stalls from which they sell snacks of all kinds. The stall-holders make distinctive noises to advertise which particular snack they are selling and, like Pavlov's dog, one quickly becomes conditioned to associate say, deep fried bananas with the sound of two bamboo sticks being struck together. Some of the snacks are not the sort of food you would prepare at home, but below I have selected recipes that are suitable. They make good snacks, buffet and cocktail food, and they also serve as side dishes to accompany main meals.

The sweet dishes given here, like the savoury snacks, may also be served as part of a large meal and would be served simultaneously with the main savoury dishes. Fresh fruit is usually served as a last course.

Fried Peanuts (Kacang Goreng)

These are delicious as a snack with drinks or as an accompaniment to a main meal.

8 oz (225 g) unsalted raw peanuts (buy the skinned variety or follow the skinning procedure given in the recipe below)

salt to taste
vegetable oil for deep frying

Heat the oil in a small but deep frying pan. Put half the peanuts into a sieve that will fit the pan. Fry the peanuts over a moderate heat, stirring for 3–5 minutes until they are golden brown. Lift the sieve with the peanuts out of the pan and allow them to drain over a bowl for a few minutes. Return the drained oil to the pan and repeat the process with the remaining peanuts. Roll the fried peanuts in absorbent kitchen paper to remove excess oil. Transfer them to a dry bowl, lightly salt them, shake well and allow to cool. Store in an airtight container. They will keep for several weeks.

Fried Peanuts with Garlic and Onion (Kacang Bawang)

Serve as a snack or a side dish. Store unused kacang bawang in an airtight container. It will keep, in an airtight container, for 2–3 weeks in a cool place.

1 lb (450 g) unsalted raw peanuts (buy the skinned variety or follow the procedure given at the beginning of the recipe)
4 cloves garlic, chopped

6 oz (175 ml) vegetable oil
2 medium onions halved and then finely sliced
salt to taste

Put the unskinned peanuts in a bowl and just cover them with boiling water. Leave them to stand for 30 minutes and then skin them by rubbing the nuts individually between thumb and finger. Line a colander with absorbent kitchen paper and put in the skinned nuts to dry. Heat the oil in a deep frying pan and add half the nuts and half the garlic. Fry them, stirring, over a moderate heat for 4 minutes or until nicely browned. Lift the peanuts out with a perforated spoon and allow them to drain through a fine sieve. Return the drained oil to the pan and repeat the process with the remaining peanuts. Fry the garlic and onion slices in the same oil until brown and crisp. Drain them through a fine sieve. Combine the peanuts, garlic and onion slices and lightly salt the mixture.

Dry Roasted Peanuts (Kacang Goreng Kering)

Roasted peanuts, as well as being eaten as a snack, are also used as an ingredient in a number of Indonesian recipes. To roast them, simply put the raw but unskinned peanuts into a heavy ungreased frying pan and cook them slowly, stirring constantly, over a low heat. The peanuts will give off a distinctive aroma when ready and the skins will darken in colour. Transfer them from the pan to a bowl and salt to taste if you wish. Or store them in an airtight container. They will keep for 2 or 3 weeks.

Pan Roasted Coconut with Peanuts (Serundeng)

Serundeng can be served as a side dish or as a garnish sprinkled over vegetables. It will keep well for 2–3 weeks in an airtight container.

3 tablespoons peanut oil *or* another good vegetable oil
1 medium onion, finely diced
2 cloves garlic, crushed
1/2 teaspoon ground cumin
2 teaspoons ground coriander
1 teaspoon prawn paste (optional)

6 oz (175 g) desiccated coconut
2 teaspoons dark brown sugar
juice of 2 lemons
salt and pepper to taste
6 fl oz (175 ml) water
4 oz (100 g) roasted *or* deep fried peanuts (see recipes above)

Heat the oil in a frying pan and add the onion, garlic, cumin, coriander and prawn paste, if used, and mix well. Stir fry the mixture for a minute or two over a moderate heat. Stir in the desiccated coconut, sugar, lemon juice and salt and pepper to taste. Stir fry the mixture for 2 or 3 minutes and then pour in the water. Continue stirring until all the water is absorbed, then cover the pan, set to simmer and leave for 45 minutes, stirring occasionally, until the coconut is nicely browned. Remove the pan from the heat and stir in the peanuts. Allow the serundeng to cool. Serve whatever amount is needed and store the rest.

Oven Roasted Coconut with Peanuts (Kacang Panggang Kelapa)

The ingredients are the same as for the recipe above, with the addition of 2 tablespoons of vegetable oil. Preheat the oven to 350° F (180° C, gas mark 4). Follow the recipe as above to the point where the water has just been added. Now transfer the contents of the pan to an ovenproof dish and pour over the top the extra 2 tablespoons of oil. Cover and bake the mixture in the preheated oven for 35–40 minutes. Stir now and again to prevent sticking and burning. Remove the dish from the oven and stir in the peanuts. Allow the mixture to cool and then serve it or store it in an airtight container.

Corn Fritters (Perkedel Jagung)

Serve as a snack or as an accompaniment to other dishes. The corn can be replaced by the same weight of roasted peanuts or fresh (shelled) or tinned shrimps or prawns (chopped).

6 oz (175 g) plain flour	1 egg
2 oz (50 g) rice flour	1/2 teaspoon prawn paste (optional)
1/2 teaspoon salt	1 clove garlic, crushed
1/2 teaspoon chilli powder	1 small onion, diced
1 teaspoon ground coriander	10 oz (500 g) fresh *or* tinned
1/2 teaspoon ground cumin	sweetcorn
4 fl oz (100 ml) water	vegetable oil for shallow frying

Put the plain flour, rice flour, salt, chilli, coriander, cumin, water, egg, prawn paste (if used) and garlic into a blender or food processor and blend to a smooth batter. Alternatively, use a mixing bowl and whisk. Transfer the batter to a bowl and mix in the onion and sweetcorn. Put enough oil in a frying pan to give a depth of 1/3 in (1/2 cm) and heat it over a medium flame. Drop in 2 tablespoons of the batter and spread it evenly to form approximately a 4-in (10-cm) circle. Fry the fritter crisp and brown on the underside and then turn it over and brown the other side. Drain the cooked fritters on absorbent kitchen paper draped over a wire rack. Repeat for all the batter. Serve or store in an airtight container. They will keep for about a week.

Spiced Beef and Coconut Balls (Serundeng Daging Sapi)

Serve as a side dish with rice and other dishes.

4 oz (100 g) desiccated coconut
2 fl oz (50 ml) water, hot
8 oz (225 g) finely minced beef
1 small onion, finely diced or
    grated
2 cloves garlic, crushed

1 teaspoon ground coriander
1/2 teaspoon ground cumin
salt and pepper to taste
1 egg, beaten
vegetable oil for shallow frying

Put the coconut in a mixing bowl and add the water. Stir well and then leave the mixture for a few minutes until all the water has been absorbed. Add the other ingredients except the oil and mix well by hand. Shape the mixture into small, firm walnut-sized balls. Heat the oil in a shallow frying pan over a moderate heat and fry the balls until they are well browned. Drain them on kitchen paper and then serve.

Savoury Peanut Fritters (Rempeyek Kacang)

These fritters are served as a snack with drinks or as an accompaniment to rice and curries. The peanuts can be replaced by the same weight of fresh or dried sweetcorn or fresh (shelled) or tinned shrimps or prawns, chopped.

1 small onion, grated
1 clove garlic, crushed
2 teaspoons ground coriander
1/2 teaspoon ground cumin
1/2 teaspoon ground turmeric
5 oz (150 g) rice flour

8 fl oz (225 ml) water *or* coconut
    milk
salt to taste
6 oz (175 g) roasted peanuts
vegetable oil for shallow frying

Put the onion, garlic, coriander, cumin, turmeric, flour and water or coconut milk into a blender and blend to a smooth batter. Transfer the batter to a bowl and add salt to taste. Stir the peanuts into the batter. Heat 2 tablespoons of oil in a shallow frying pan, drop in 3–4 tablespoon amounts of peanut batter and spread it evenly by tilting the pan back and forth. The batter does not need to cover the whole surface of the pan. Fry until brown and crisp on the underside. Turn over and brown the other side. Drain on absorbent paper draped over a wire rack. Repeat for all the batter. Serve or store in an airtight container. These fritters will keep for about a week.

Meat and Potato Balls
(Perkedel Kentang Daging Sapi)

Small deep fried meat and potato balls. They are eaten hot or cold as a
snack food. If rolled very small they can also be used as a garnish for
other dishes.

1 lb (450 g) potatoes
vegetable oil for deep frying
2 small onions, finely diced
2 cloves garlic
8 oz (225 g) finely minced beef
1/2 teaspoon nutmeg

salt and pepper to taste
1 tablespoon fresh parsley, finely
   chopped
4 spring onions, finely chopped
2 eggs, separated

Boil the potatoes in their skins until tender. When cooked, peel and
mash them. During the time the potatoes are cooking, heat 2
tablespoons of oil in a frying pan and sauté the onions and garlic until
lightly browned. Stir in the meat, nutmeg, salt and pepper to taste and
fry the mixture, stirring, for one minute. Mash the potatoes and
combine with the mixture, then add the parsley and spring onions.
Beat in the egg yolks and then shape the mixture into walnut-sized
balls (smaller if they are to be used as a garnish). Heat enough oil for
deep frying in a wok or deep pan. Dip the meatballs in the egg white
and then deep fry batches of them until they turn golden brown. Drain
the finished meatballs on absorbent paper and serve.

Fried Wun–Tun (Pangsit)

Pangsit are small deep-fried dumplings filled with a pork- or prawn-
based stuffing. The pastry is very thin and the same as that used by the
Chinese to make wonton. Wonton skins can be bought in most
Chinese grocery stores. There are usually about 90 skins to 1 lb
(450 g).

Filling 1: Pork and Prawns

2 tablespoons oil
1 medium onion, finely diced
2 cloves garlic
4 oz tinned *or* shelled prawns *or*
   shrimps, minced or finely
   chopped

8 oz (225 g) pork, minced
1/2-in (1-cm) piece root ginger,
   peeled and finely chopped
1 tablespoon dark soya sauce
2 eggs
salt and pepper to taste

Filling 2: Chicken and Prawns

This is the same as for filling 1 but replace the onion with 2 young leeks, finely chopped, and the pork with 8 oz (225 g) minced chicken. For both fillings, lightly brown the onion (or leek) and garlic in the oil and then combine them with all the other ingredients and mix well.

Pastry Skin for Wrapping

either	*or*
8 oz (225 g) plain flour	8 oz (225 g) wonton skins
salt to taste	*plus*
2 small eggs	oil for deep frying
water as required	1 egg white

To make the pastry: sift the flour and salt into a mixing bowl. Beat the eggs into the flour and add enough water to form a firm but pliable dough. Knead well by hand or in a food processor for 5 minutes. Dust a board with flour and roll out a portion of the dough into as thin a sheet as possible. Cut this sheet into 4-in (10-cm) squares and set them aside. Repeat for all the dough. Alternatively, use shop-bought wonton skins. Place a small tablespoon of filling onto a square of pastry and fold the corners over to make a triangle. Seal the edges by pressing hard with your fingers (use a little egg white to make a good joint if necessary) and repeat for all the filling and dough. Heat the oil in a deep frying pan or wok and deep fry the pangsits a few at a time until crisp and golden brown (2–3 minutes). Drain and serve hot or cool.

Banana Fritters (Pisang Goreng)

Banana fritters are a very popular snack food in Indonesia. They are made in a variety of ways and I have given three different recipes here. In the first the bananas are dipped in a flour and egg batter and deep fried. In the second they are dipped in a coconut milk and rice flour batter and shallow fried and in the third, simply sprinkled with lemon juice and sugar before deep frying. Serve the fried bananas on their own as a snack, as a dessert or as part of a large meal alongside savoury dishes.

Method 1: Bananas Deep Fried in Batter

4 bananas, medium-sized, firm but
  ripe
4 oz (100 g) white flour
pinch of salt
8 fl oz (225 ml) water

1 egg
oil for deep frying
icing sugar to taste
cinnamon to taste

Peel the bananas and cut them lengthwise in two. Beat the flour, salt, water and egg together to form a smooth batter. Heat the oil for deep frying. Dip the halved bananas in the batter and deep fry them until golden brown in the hot oil. Drain on absorbent paper and serve dusted with icing sugar and sprinkled with cinnamon.

Variation: Dice the bananas and then mix them with the batter. Drop tablespoons of this mixture into the hot oil and deep fry until golden brown.

Method 2: Bananas Shallow Fried in Batter

4 bananas, medium-sized, ripe but
  firm
8 fl oz (225 ml) fresh *or* canned
  coconut milk (see page 15 for
  preparation from desiccated
  coconut) *or* 8 fl oz (225 ml) milk
4 oz (100 g) rice flour

pinch of salt
1 oz (25 g) butter, melted
vegetable oil *or* butter for shallow
  frying
icing sugar to taste
cinnamon to taste

Cut the bananas in two lengthwise and, if they are too big for your frying pan, in two crosswise. Combine the coconut milk or milk, rice flour, salt and melted butter and beat the mixture to a smooth batter. Dip the banana pieces in the batter and shallow fry them in hot oil, or butter, on both sides until nicely browned. Dust with icing sugar and sprinkle with cinnamon before serving.

Method 3: Deep Fried Bananas

4 bananas, just ripe, halved and
  sliced into halves lengthwise
2 oz (50 g) brown sugar

juice of 1 lemon
oil for deep frying

Put the halved bananas in a bowl, sprinkle them with sugar and lemon juice, cover and set them aside for 30 minutes. Heat the oil in a deep frying pan or wok over a moderate flame and carefully place the banana halves in it a few at a time. Deep fry them until golden brown, drain on absorbent paper and serve.

Banana Pancakes (Panekuk Pisang)

2 eggs, beaten
1/2 teaspoon salt
4 oz (100 g) plain flour
10 fl oz (275 ml) milk *or* fresh *or* canned coconut milk

1 tablespoon white sugar
2 medium-sized bananas, peeled and mashed
vegetable oil *or* butter for frying
lemon juice to taste

Beat the eggs and salt together in a mixing bowl. Whisk in the flour and then the milk to form a smooth batter. Stir in the sugar and bananas and beat the mixture well to eliminate any large lumps of banana. Alternatively, the ingredients of the batter could be put into the container of a food blender or processor and beaten until smooth. Brush a heavy pan with butter or oil and heat it over a moderate flame. Pour some batter into the pan and swirl it around to form a thin 1/4-in (1/2-cm) coating on the surface of the pan. Lightly brown the bottom side of the pancake and then turn it over and brown the other side. Repeat for the remaining batter, pile the cooked pancakes on top of one another on a buttered plate and then serve them sprinkled with lemon juice.

Coconut Filled Pancakes (Semar Mendem)

Batter

2 eggs, beaten
1/2 teaspoon salt
4 oz (100 g) plain flour
10 fl oz (275 ml) milk *or* fresh *or* canned coconut milk
vegetable oil *or* butter for shallow frying

Filling

4 oz (100 g) brown sugar
8 fl oz (225 ml) water
6 oz (175 g) desiccated coconut *or* fresh coconut, grated
1/2 teaspoon vanilla essence (optional)
juice of 1/2 lemon

To make the batter, put the eggs and salt into a bowl and beat them together. Stir in the flour and then the milk and beat the mixture to form a smooth batter. Set it aside, covered. To make the filling, heat and stir the sugar and water in a pan until the sugar is dissolved. Add the coconut and vanilla essence, if used, and simmer, stirring, until all the liquid has been absorbed by the coconut. Stir in the lemon juice and set the mixture aside. Brush a heavy frying pan with butter or oil and heat it over a moderate flame. Pour some batter into the pan and swirl it around to form a thin coating over the surface of the pan. Lightly brown the bottom side of the pancake and then turn it over and brown the other side. Repeat for the remaining batter. Pile the cooked pancakes one on top of the other on a buttered plate. Now fill each one with the filling, roll it up and serve hot or cool.

Avocado Dessert (Buah Avokat)

In Indonesia avocados are treated as a fruit and as such are eaten as a dessert. Choose quite ripe ones, one per person, cut them in 2 and remove the stone. Place the two halves on individual small plates and serve them sprinkled with lemon juice and brown sugar.

RICE AND NOODLES
(Nasi and Mi)

RICE (Nasi)

Some of the best rice in the world is grown in Indonesia and in particular in Java and Bali. The rice paddies which represent the wealth of a village community are carefully cultivated and the quality of the rice produced is a matter of pride as well as finance to the farmers. Many varieties are grown, including a black rice that makes a tasty and exotic rice pudding. Rice is essential to Indonesian meals.

As in all countries where rice is a staple food, numerous ways have been developed to cook it, but they are all really variations of two basic techniques. Firstly, there is the absorption method in which the rice is boiled in just the amount of water needed to cook it perfectly, and secondly, the steaming method in which the rice is first parboiled and then steamed. The cooked rice should not be soggy, it should be slightly fluffy and in separate grains (unless you are using one of the glutinous sticky dessert rices). Patna long grain rice is the best to use. Branded varieties can be used straight from the packet but loose, unbranded rice should be washed in running cold water until the water runs clear, before cooking. The exact proportion of rice to cooking water is a matter of judgement and of experimentation but as a general rule, 1 volume of rice to 2 volumes of water will be about right. Salt is not normally added to rice in Indonesia but since many people prefer their rice with salt, I have left it up to you in the recipes. The Indonesian way of serving rice is in a large communal bowl.

Boiled Rice (Nasi Putih)

Method 1

Serves 4–6

1 lb (450 g) long grain rice
2 volumes of water to 1 volume
    rice
salt (optional)

Measure the rice by cupfuls into a sieve or colander and rinse it under cold water until the water runs clear. Drain the rice and transfer it to a heavy-bottomed pan with a tight fitting lid. (You can improve the fit of a lid by wrapping it in aluminium foil.) Add 2 volumes more water than rice and salt, if it is being used. Cover the pan and bring the rice to the boil over a high heat. Now stir the rice with the handle end of a wooden spoon, then cover it again, reduce the heat to very low and leave it to simmer for 15–20 minutes. At this stage the rice should just be tender. Don't lift the lid off to check or you will lose some of the steam; the timing has to be guessed at first. Remove the pan from the heat and leave it to stand, still covered, for 5 minutes. The rice is now ready to be served.

If you find that the rice tends to stick to the bottom of your pan, stand the pan on a wet cloth for the last 5 minutes. To loosen encrusted rice from the pan, put some water and potato peelings into the empty pan and boil them for a few minutes. The rice crust can then be cleaned off.

Method 2

Serves 4–6

This method is slightly quicker than method 1 but it requires more care.

1 lb (450 g) long grain rice
1½ volumes of water to the
    volume of rice
salt (optional)

Measure the rice by cupfuls into a sieve or colander and rinse it under cold water until the water runs clear. Drain the rice and transfer it to a heavy-bottomed pan with a tight fitting lid. Add 1½ volumes of water and the salt if it is being used. Bring the rice to the boil and leave it to bubble, uncovered, over a moderate heat until all the water has been absorbed. Do not stir. Now cover the pan and leave it for 10–12 minutes on a very low heat. The rice should then be ready.

Boiled and Steamed Rice (Nasi Putih)

Serves 4–6

The Indonesians have a proper rice steamer for this process but a colander with a lid on top, placed over a pan containing a little water, is a good substitute.

1 lb (450 g) long grain rice
1 pint (550 ml) water
salt (optional)

Rinse the rice under cold running water until the water runs clear. Drain the rice and transfer it to a heavy-bottomed pan. Add the water and salt, if used, and bring the rice to the boil. Reduce the heat and gently boil the rice, uncovered, until the water has been absorbed. The rice will be partially cooked now. Transfer it to a steamer or colander over a pan containing 1–2 in (2–5 cm) of water. Cover the rice and steam it by allowing the water in the steamer or pan to boil for about 10 minutes. The rice, when ready to serve, should be tender with no hard centre, but with sufficient texture to have remained in separate grains.

Variation: Replace the water in which you partially cook the rice, with the same volume of fresh or canned coconut milk. (For preparation from desiccated coconut see page 15.) This type of rice is called nasi uduk.

Yellow Rice with Coconut Milk (Nasi Kuning)

Serves 4–6

Rice coloured yellow with turmeric and cooked in coconut milk instead of water is a bright, rich centre-piece to a special meal. The finished rice should be colourfully garnished.

1 lb (450 g) long grain rice, washed several times and drained
1 pint (550 ml) fresh *or* canned coconut milk
1 teaspoon ground turmeric
1 bay leaf *or* daun salem leaf
1/2 teaspoon salt

To garnish
choose from:
onion flakes, fried brown
finely sliced cucumber
fresh chilli peppers, deseeded and chopped

Put the rice in a bowl, cover it with water and leave it to soak for 2–3 hours. Drain it and then put the rice with the other ingredients into a heavy-bottomed pan. Bring the rice to a gentle boil and cook it over a low heat, uncovered, until all the coconut milk has been absorbed. Now stir the rice with the handle end of a wooden spoon and then cover the pot with a tightly fitting lid (see method 1 for boiling rice on page 64). Reduce the heat to the lowest setting possible and gently cook the rice for another 15 minutes. The rice is now ready to tip into a serving bowl, garnish and serve.

Yellow Rice with Spices (Nasi Kuning Bumbu)

Serves 4–6

1 lb (450 g) long grain rice, washed several times and drained
2 tablespoons vegetable oil
1 small onion, finely diced
1 teaspoon ground turmeric
1 teaspoon ground coriander
1/2 teaspoon ground cumin
1/2 teaspoon cinnamon
salt to taste
1 pint (550 ml) water, boiling

Put the rice in a bowl, cover it with water and leave it to soak for 2–3 hours. Drain it then set the rice aside. Heat the vegetable oil in a heavy-bottomed pan and stir fry the onion in it until softened. Add the spices and salt and sauté the mixture for another minute. Stir the rice into the pan and sauté the rice and spices for 2–3 minutes. Pour in the boiling water and cook the rice over a moderate heat until the water is absorbed. Stir the rice with the handle end of a wooden spoon and cover the pot with a tightly fitting lid (see boiled rice method 1 on page 64.) Reduce the heat to very low, gently cook the rice for another 15 minutes and then serve.

Rice Cooked in Coconut Milk (Nasi Santan)

Serves 4–6

1 lb (450 g) long grain rice, washed several times and drained
1 1/2 pints (700 ml) water *or* 16 fl oz (450 ml) water and 8 fl oz (225 ml) coconut milk
4 oz (100 g) desiccated coconut
1 teaspoon grated lemon peel *or* chopped lemon grass
salt to taste

Put the rice in a heavy-bottomed pan, add the water or water and coconut milk mixture, the desiccated coconut, lemon peel or lemon grass and add a little salt to taste. Bring the rice to the boil, stir well and gently boil it until all the liquid has been absorbed. Cover the pan with a tightly-fitting lid (see boiled rice method 1 on page 64) and reduce the heat to very low. Simmer for 15–20 minutes. Serve hot and garnish it as for yellow rice with coconut milk on page 65.

Sticky Rice (Ketan)

Sticky or glutinous rice, as its name implies, is more starchy than ordinary rice and, as a result, the cooked rice grains stick to each other. The rice used is normally a short-grained variety and although sticky rice is used for savoury dishes (particularly in those dishes in which stickiness is an advantage, such as rice rolls or rice stuffed banana leaves), it is more popular for desserts. Glutinous or sticky rice can be substituted for long grain rice in any of the above recipes but it is generally cooked by the boiling and steaming method. Follow the recipe exactly as for long grain rice. Sticky rice is normally available in Chinese grocery stores.

Fried Rice

Fried rice is quick to make and the recipe is open to any number of variations from the very basic to the most elaborate. Cooked rice is fried with spices and a combination of one or more other ingredients, including vegetables, shellfish, meat or poultry. Because the combination of ingredients used in making fried rice very much depends on what is available and on the cook's taste, I have given two general rather than specific recipes. The first recipe is for simple fried rice to give you an idea of the method and the second is for a far more elaborate dish in which a large number of ingredients are suggested and you can make a choice about which ones to select. Boiled rice used in the preparation of nasi goreng should be made a couple of hours before it is needed and then allowed to cool. The rice should not be soggy so when you boil it be careful not to overcook it or to use too much water.

Simple Fried Rice (Nasi Goreng)
Serves 2–4

This basic recipe can be built upon to include other spices, fish, meat, poultry, vegetables, nuts and garnishes as shown in the following recipe.

2 tablespoons vegetable oil
1 medium onion, sliced
1 clove garlic, crushed
1 or 2 fresh *or* dried red chillies,
   finely chopped *or* 1/2-1 teaspoon
   chilli powder
1 lb (450 g) cooked rice
1 tablespoon dark soya sauce
1/2 teaspoon brown sugar
salt to taste

To garnish
select from:
tomato wedges
cucumber slices
thin omelettes cut into strips *or* 1
   freshly fried egg per person

Heat the oil in a heavy frying pan or wok, add the onion, garlic and chillies and stir fry them for about 1 minute. Add the rice, soya sauce and brown sugar. Mix well and cook, stirring the mixture continuously over a moderate heat for 5–6 minutes. During this time check the rice for seasoning and add salt if needed. If the mixture starts to look too dry, add a little more vegetable oil (in Indonesia they also add a beaten egg). Serve the fried rice immediately on a large serving dish or on individual plates and garnish it with tomato wedges and/or cucumber slices and/or omelette strips, or 1 freshly fried egg per person.

Special Fried Rice (Nasi Goreng Istimewa)

Serves 6

2 fl oz (50 ml) vegetable oil
2 medium onions, chopped
2 cloves garlic, crushed
2 fresh *or* dried red chillies, finely
   chopped *or* 1 teaspoon chilli
   powder
1 teaspoon prawn paste (optional)
1 1/2 lb (700 g) cooked rice
2 tablespoons soya sauce
2 teaspoons brown sugar
salt and pepper to taste

plus
1 1/2 lb (700 g) of one or a
   combination of the following:

chicken, cooked and cubed
pork, cooked and cubed
ham, cubed

prawns, shrimps, shelled and fried
   tender
beef, cooked and cubed
peanuts, roasted
cashew nuts, roasted
mushrooms, sliced

To garnish
select from:
tomato wedges
cucumber, sliced and diced
celery, chopped
fried peanuts
fried onion flakes
prawn crackers,
chopped ham, thin omelette strips
   or 1 freshly fried egg per person

Heat the oil in a large, heavy frying pan or wok. Add the onions, garlic and chillies or chilli powder and stir fry for 1–2 minutes. Stir in the prawn paste (if used) and fry for a further minute. Add the combination of the other ingredients that you have chosen and stir well. Continue stirring and frying the mixture until all the ingredients are thoroughly heated through. Now add the rice, soya sauce, brown sugar and salt and pepper to taste. Stir and fry the rice continuously for 4–6 minutes or until all the rice grains are coated with oil and any uncooked ingredients are tender. Add more oil (in Indonesia they also add a beaten egg) if the rice starts to dry out. Serve the fried rice immediately on a large serving dish and decorate it with a combination of selected garnishes.

Spiced Rice (Nasi Gemuk)

Serves 2–4

The Indonesian name means rice cooked in oil and in this method spices are fried in oil, raw rice is stirred in and then water or coconut milk is added and the mixture simmered until the rice is cooked.

3 tablespoons vegetable oil
1-in (2.5-cm) piece of cinnamon
1 clove
2 cardamom pods, broken open
1 small onion, finely diced
2 cloves garlic, crushed
1/2-in (1-cm) piece root ginger, finely chopped

1/2 teaspoon ground coriander
1 lb (450 g) long grain rice washed several times and drained
salt to taste
1 1/4 pints (700 ml) water *or* stock *or* fresh *or* canned coconut milk

Heat the oil in a heavy saucepan or wok and add the cinnamon, clove and cardamoms. Fry for 1 or 2 minutes. Add the onion, garlic, ginger root and coriander and stir fry for another 1 or 2 minutes. Stir the rice into the spice mixture. Salt to taste. Carefully pour in the water, stock or coconut milk (traditionally used) and bring the rice to the boil. Cover, reduce the heat and simmer the rice for 15–20 minutes or until it is tender.

Variation: If you like chilli hot dishes, add 1 or 2 finely chopped chillies along with the onion and garlic.

Sweet Smelling Coconut Rice (Nasi Gurih)

Serves 2–4

Serve this delicious rice with meat, chicken or fish dishes. It is simple to prepare and lends an exotic aroma to a meal.

1¼ pints (700 ml) fresh *or* canned coconut milk
1½ teaspoons salt
¼ teaspoon freshly ground black pepper
¼ teaspoon ground cloves

½ teaspoon nutmeg
½ teaspoon cinnamon
1 teaspoon grated lemon rind *or* chopped lemon grass
1 bay leaf *or* daun salem leaf
1 lb (450 g) long grain rice

Put all the ingredients except the rice into a heavy saucepan and bring the mixture to a gentle boil, stirring constantly. Add the rice and bring it to a very slow boil, stirring. Cover the pan with a tightly fitting lid, reduce the heat and simmer for 20 minutes. Remove the pan from the heat, stir and then set aside, off the heat, for 5 minutes before serving.

Festive Rice Cone (Nasi Tumpeng)

Serves 8

One of the dishes always seen at an Indonesian celebration or festivity is a conical shaped mound of yellow rice beautifully decorated with a variety of foods ranging from flower-shaped chillies to whole roast chickens. Here is a recipe for the rice cone and some suggestions for garnishes. The quantities given will make rice for up to 8 people and the recipe is excellent as a party dish.

2 tablespoons vegetable oil
1 large onion, finely diced
2 cloves garlic, crushed
2 lb (1 kg) long grain white rice, washed and drained
1½ pints (850 ml) water
1½ pints (850 ml) fresh *or* canned coconut milk
1 teaspoon grated lemon rind *or* chopped lemon grass
4 bay leaves *or* daun salem leaves
2 teaspoons ground turmeric
3 teaspoons salt

To garnish
select from:
fresh red chillies, cut into flower shapes (see method below)
fresh green chillies, seeded, cut into strips
marbled eggs (see page 51)
strips of omelette
roasted peanuts
cucumber slices
prawn crackers
meatballs (see page 81)
prawnballs
salad vegetables, chopped or shredded

Heat the oil in a heavy saucepan and sauté the onion and garlic until golden. Add the rice and stir it over the heat for a couple of minutes. Slowly pour in the water and then the coconut milk. Mix well and add the lemon rind or lemon grass, bay leaves or daun salem leaves, turmeric and salt. Bring the rice to the boil slowly, stirring constantly. Cover the pan with a tightly-fitting lid and gently simmer for 20 minutes. Remove the pan from the heat, stir the contents and then set the pan aside, off the heat, for 5 minutes. The rice is now ready. Arrange it in a cone shape (a conical shaped sieve is good for helping to do this) on a serving dish and garnish.

Note: To make chilli flowers, slit the chillies two or three times vertically from tip almost to stem. Drop them into iced water and the strips will curl.

NOODLES (Mi)

Noodles are an important ingredient of Indonesian cooking. They are made from wheat or rice flour, and are made both with and without eggs, in almost as many shapes and varieties as Italian pasta. Noodles are usually served in one of three ways: boiled in a soup (mi godog), fried (mi goreng) or fried and then boiled in stock (mi goreng knah). In each case, other ingredients in the recipe would include a combination of vegetables, fish, meat and spices.

It is usually more convenient to buy noodles rather than make them. Cooking instructions for noodles are, as a rule, given on the packets in which they are sold and it is most important to follow these carefully, since the success of a noodle recipe depends on the noodles not being over or under cooked. Perfectly cooked noodles should be just soft on the outside going to just firm in the middle. Noodles which are to be fried are first boiled and then fried and in this instance it's important to drain, oil and air the noodles once they are cooked and before frying. This prevents them from overcooking in their own heat and keeps the texture firm, which is important for frying.

Noodles in Chicken Soup (Mi Ayam Godog)

Serves 4

The method described in this recipe is a general one and where I have given chicken as the main ingredient you may substitute 1 lb (450 g) beef, pork or prawns or any combination of meat, poultry or shellfish. Similarly where I have given cabbage and beansprouts you may use other vegetables such as broccoli, carrots, spinach, mushrooms and so on.

2 tablespoons oil
1 small onion, sliced
2 cloves garlic, crushed
2 pints (1 litre) water
1-in (2.5-cm) piece of root ginger,
  finely chopped
2 chicken legs *or* breasts
salt and black pepper to taste
3 oz (75 g) cabbage leaves,
  shredded
1–2 fresh *or* dried red chillies finely
  chopped (optional)

2 oz (50 g) beansprouts, washed
4 spring onions, chopped
12 oz (350 g) egg noodles
dark soya sauce to taste

To garnish
select from:
sliced hard-boiled eggs
thin strips omelette
tomato wedges
chopped celery tops
fried onion flakes or rings

Heat the oil in a large saucepan and add the onion and garlic. Stir fry until the onion is softened. Add the water, ginger, chicken and salt and black pepper to taste. Bring the mixture to the boil, reduce the heat, cover and simmer until the chicken is tender, about 45 minutes. Remove the chicken pieces from the pan, allow them to cool and then bone and shred the meat. Meanwhile, leave the stock on a low simmer. Add the cabbage leaves and chillies (if used) and shredded chicken to the simmering stock, increase the heat and bring the mixture to a gentle boil. Add the beansprouts, spring onions and noodles. Loosen the strands of the noodles with a fork and stir in soya sauce to taste. Adjust the seasoning and simmer the soup, covered, for 5–7 minutes or until the noodles are cooked. Transfer the contents of the pan to a serving dish and garnish before serving.

Variations

1. For a quick noodle soup leave out the chicken and use chicken stock or a stock cube to make the broth.
2. Meatballs (pre-cooked in boiling water) may be added to a quick noodle soup to make it more substantial or to the noodle soup with chicken for a more elaborate dish. (See page 81 for meatball recipe.)

Fried Noodles with Beef and Prawns (Mi Goreng Sapi)

Serves 4

The method described in this recipe is a general one and where I have given cooked beef and prawns as ingredients you may substitute cooked chicken or pork or a combination of all four of them. Similarly, where I have given broccoli and celery you may use other vegetables such as carrots, beansprouts, Chinese cabbage, mushrooms and so on.

8 oz (225 g) noodles
3 tablespoons oil
1 medium onion, diced
2 cloves garlic, crushed
1-in (2.5-cm) piece root ginger,
  finely chopped
4 oz (100 g) broccoli, chopped
2 sticks celery, chopped
8 oz (225 g) cooked beef, cubed
4 oz (100 g) cooked prawns *or*
  shrimps

dark soya sauce to taste
4 spring onions, chopped
salt and pepper to taste

To garnish
select from:
fried onion flakes
1–2 fresh *or* dried red chillies,
  finely chopped
fresh parsley, finely chopped
thin omelette strips

Drop the noodles in lots of boiling water and cook them until they are just tender. Drain them and immediately toss them in 1 tablespoon oil; set them aside. Heat the remaining oil in a large heavy frying pan or wok and fry the onion, garlic and ginger until the onion is softened. Add the broccoli and celery and stir fry for 2–3 minutes. Stir in the beef and prawns or shrimps, mix well and heat the whole mixture through. Stir in the noodles then fry and stir them over a low heat for 2–3 minutes. Add the soya sauce and spring onions, season to taste with salt and pepper and stir fry for another minute or two. Serve the fried noodles in individual bowls or in a tureen and garnish.

Variation: Uncooked beef, prawns, pork or chicken may be used in this recipe. Simply cut the uncooked ingredients into thin, bite-sized pieces and fry them with the onion, garlic and ginger until tender. Then proceed as directed in the recipe.

Braised Noodles (Mi Goreng Kuah)

Serves 4

Fried noodles prepared as above are covered in hot soup stock, brought to the boil, garnished and served. Follow the fried noodle recipe to the point where the noodles are fried and ready to be removed from the frying pan. Now pour over them 8 fl oz (225 ml) hot soup stock. Bring to the boil and boil for 1 minute before serving. Serve the braised noodles in individual bowls or in a tureen and garnish.

MEAT DISHES
(Masakan Daging)

Indonesians enjoy variations of taste, texture and colour within the same meal and do not like the taste of any one dish to dominate. Because of this, and because meat is relatively expensive, the meat course in an Indonesian meal is less important in terms of quantity than it might be in the West. However, its taste is important and Indonesian meat recipes are delicious. Spices and other ingredients are combined in ways which may seem unusual to Western taste buds. Indeed, Indonesian meat and chicken recipes perhaps best illustrate the fusion of indigenous Arab and Chinese cooking styles which is unique to Indonesian cuisine.

The recipes I have given here are mainly for beef, lamb or mutton with a few pork recipes but most of them can be adapted to suit cuts and types of meat other than those suggested. In Indonesia, beef, mutton, lamb, buffalo and goat are all readily available. The meat tends to be quite tough and is used in small quantities, thinly sliced or cubed.

At the end of the chapter there is a section on sate dishes. To prepare sate, cubes of meat, chicken or seafood are skewered on bamboo sticks, marinated, grilled and then dipped in a thick, usually peanut sauce. Sate is very popular in Indonesia and is one of the dishes most associated with it and also with Singapore and Malaysia.

Spicy Lamb or Beef Stew in Soya Sauce (Semur Daging)

Serves 4

Serve with rice or noodles and a salad or a vegetable dish.

2 tablespoons oil
2 medium onions, finely sliced
2 cloves garlic, crushed
1-in (2.5-cm) root ginger, chopped
   or 1/2 teaspoon ground ginger
1 lb (450 g) beef *or* lamb cut into
   small cubes or slices

2 medium tomatoes, sliced and
   chopped
2 tablespoons dark soya sauce
1/2 tablespoon dark brown sugar
1/4 teaspoon nutmeg
1/2 teaspoon cinnamon
pepper to taste
4 fl oz (100 ml) water

Heat the oil in a saucepan and add the onion, garlic and ginger root (if ground ginger is used, add it later with the nutmeg). Stir fry until the onion is lightly browned. Add the meat cubes or slices and gently brown them all over. Add the tomatoes and fry them with the beef for 1–2 minutes. Combine all the remaining ingredients and add the mixture to the pan. Bring the pan to the boil, reduce heat, cover and simmer for about 30 minutes or until the meat is tender.

Variation 1: To make the dish spicy hot, add 1 or 2 finely chopped chillies at the same time as the meat.

Variation 2: To make the dish more substantial add 1 large potato, sliced only 1/4 in (0.5 cm) thick, with the tomatoes, fry the potato slices with the beef and tomatoes until lightly browned and then proceed as directed in the recipe.

Marinated Braised Beef or Lamb Slices in Soya Sauce (Lapis Daging)

Serves 4

Serve piping hot with boiled rice and sambals.

1 lb (450 g) beef *or* lamb, thinly
   sliced and cut into 2-in (5-cm)
   squares
2 medium onions, 1 finely diced
   and 1 sliced
2 cloves garlic, crushed

3 tablespoons dark soya sauce
pepper to taste
1/4 teaspoon nutmeg
1 teaspoon cinnamon
2 tablespoons oil
2 medium tomatoes, chopped

Combine the beef or lamb, diced onion, garlic, soya sauce, pepper, nutmeg and cinnamon in a bowl, stir well and leave the meat to marinate in the mixture for 1 hour or longer. Heat the oil in a saucepan and stir fry the sliced onion until lightly browned. Add the meat and marinade to the pan, mix well and cook, stirring, for 2 minutes. Add the tomatoes, reduce the heat to low, cover the pan and cook for 30 minutes or until the meat is tender.

Dry Fried Sweet Spiced Beef (Daging Manis)

Serves 4

Daging manis may be served hot or cool. It's good both as a snack and with boiled rice and vegetables as a main meal.

1 lb (450 g) lean beef, thinly sliced, cut into 2-in (5-cm) squares	1 tablespoon dark brown sugar
1/2 teaspoon hot pepper sauce	1 teaspoon salt
1 teaspoon coriander seeds, crushed	1 teaspoon prawn *or* shrimp paste (optional)
1/2 teaspoon cumin seeds, crushed	2 tablespoons oil
1 teaspoon finely grated root ginger *or* 1 teaspoon ground ginger	1 small onion, finely diced
	1 tablespoon tamarind water *or* 1 tablespoon lemon juice
	12 fl oz (350 ml) water or stock

Combine the beef, hot pepper sauce, coriander, cumin, ginger, salt and sugar and prawn paste (if used) in a bowl. Mix them well together and ensure that the beef slices are well covered in the marinade. Leave the beef to marinate for 1 hour or longer. Heat the oil in a frying pan or wok and stir fry the onion until it is light brown. Add the beef and the marinade and fry the beef on both sides until just browned. Add the tamarind water or lemon juice and water or stock and bring the pan to the boil. Reduce the heat to very low, cover the pan and gently simmer the beef for 30 minutes. Now remove the pan lid and continue to cook the beef over a low heat until all the liquid in the pan has evaporated, taking care that the meat does not char.

Dried Spiced Beef (Dendeng)

Serves 4 or more

Dendeng is prepared from dry fried sweet spiced beef (daging manis) which is prepared by following the recipe above. The dried beef is dried even further by slow roasting it in the oven to give slightly crisp, spicy slices of meat. Dendeng stored in an airtight container in the fridge will keep for 2–3 months. It is full of flavour and small amounts added to milder dishes will brighten them up. Dendeng can also be reheated by frying or grilling and served with rice and sambals.

Prepare dry fried spiced sweet beef as in the recipe above. Preheat the oven to 250° F (130° C, gas mark ½). Place the beef slices side by side on a flat baking sheet and put them in the oven. Roast the meat for 1 hour, turning the slices over every 15 minutes. The finished dendeng should be dark brown in colour and slightly crisp, but not burnt.

Crisp Fried Meat and Coconut (Dendeng Ragi)

Serves 6–8

Dendeng ragi is served on its own as a savoury or as a side dish with rice and/or vegetables. It is very tasty and keeps well.

2 fl oz (50 ml) oil
1 small onion, finely diced
2 cloves garlic, crushed
1 lb (450 g) lean beef, thinly sliced
6 oz (175 g) desiccated coconut
1 teaspoon pepper

1 tablespoon lemon juice
1 teaspoon ground cumin
2 teaspoons ground coriander
1 tablespoon dark brown sugar
salt to taste

Sauté the onion and garlic in the oil in a large pan until softened. Add the meat slices and cook, stirring, until both sides are lightly browned. Add the remaining ingredients and mix well. Cover the pan and simmer gently, stirring now and again, until the meat is tender (about 30 minutes). Remove the pan lid and continue to cook until the mixture is very dry. Stir occasionally to prevent any sticking. Serve hot or store the dendeng ragi in an airtight jar in the refrigerator. It will keep for 2–3 weeks. Serve cold or heat it by refrying or grilling.

Meat Balinese Style (Daging Masak Bali)

Serves 4

This is a simple but effective recipe. It is very hot but if you prefer less spicy food, reduce the number of chillies used in the recipe. Beef is used in this recipe, but lamb, mutton or pork can be substituted. The recipe may also be used for cooked meats and it provides an unusual way of using up left-over roast beef or ham. Serve hot with boiled rice and vegetables.

3–4 fresh *or* dried red chillies
1 medium onion, chopped
3 cloves garlic
1-in (2.5-cm) piece root ginger, chopped
1 teaspoon prawn *or* shrimp paste (optional)
2 tablespoons oil

1 lb (450 g) lean beef, thinly sliced and cut into strips
6 fl oz (175 ml) water, boiling
2 tablespoons dark soya sauce
1 teaspoon dark brown sugar
juice of 1 lemon
salt to taste

Put the chillies, onion, garlic, root ginger, prawn paste (if used) and oil into a blender and blend them to a paste. Alternatively, dice the chillies, onion, garlic and ginger as finely as possible and pound them to a paste with the oil and prawn paste using a pestle and mortar. Add the paste to a wok or frying pan over a moderate heat and stir fry if for 3–4 minutes. Add the meat strips and continue to stir fry, turning the meat now and again, until the meat is lightly browned on both sides. Pour in the boiling water, soya sauce, sugar and lemon juice, stir well, season to taste with salt, cover and simmer over a low heat until the beef is tender (about 30 minutes; however, if you are using pre-cooked meat, this simmering time will be about 6 minutes). Uncover the pan and continue cooking until almost all the liquid has evaporated.

Beef Javanese Style (Empal Daging)

Serves 4

A piece of any cheaper cut of beef is gently boiled until tender. It is then sliced 1/3 in (1/2 cm) thick and fried in a rich spicy mixture and finally simmered in a little soya sauce and stock or coconut milk.

1 lb (450 g) stewing beef
2 tablespoons oil
1 medium onion, finely diced
2 cloves garlic, crushed
pepper to taste

1 teaspoon ground coriander powder
1 teaspoon finely chopped lemon rind *or* lemon grass
2 tablespoons soya sauce

Place the beef in one piece in a saucepan, just cover with water, bring to the boil, cover with a lid, reduce the heat and simmer for about 1 hour or until the meat is just tender. Skim off any scum that forms. Leave the meat and stock to cool. Meanwhile, heat the oil in a wok or frying pan and add the onion, garlic, pepper, coriander and lemon rind or lemon grass and stir fry until the onions are softened. Thinly slice the meat and then add it to the pan. Fry the slices, turning them occasionally, over a moderate heat for 5 minutes. Stir in the soya sauce and 2 fl oz (50 ml) of the stock in which the meat was cooked. Add salt to taste and cook the meat over a low heat until all the liquid has been absorbed or evaporated. The empal is now ready to serve.

Variation: Replace the soya sauce and stock by 4 fl oz (100 ml) coconut milk. Or alternatively, omit the soya sauce and simply fry the meat slices gently in the spices until cooked.

Beef Semarang Style (Lapis Daging Semarang)

Serves 4

Thin slices of beef are marinated in a spicy sweet mixture, fried and then simmered with tomatoes and the marinade, until tender.

1 lb (450 g) rump, topside *or* round steak, thinly sliced in rounds	3 tablespoons dark soya sauce
	1/2 teaspoon nutmeg
	1 tablespoon dark brown sugar
1 medium onion, chopped	2 tablespoons oil
3 cloves garlic	2 medium ripe tomatoes, peeled
1 teaspoon freshly ground black pepper	and chopped

Gently beat the meat slices with a mallet to thin them out. Put the onion, garlic, pepper, soya sauce, nutmeg and sugar into a blender and blend the mixture to a smooth paste. Add a little water if necessary, to keep the blades turning. Put the beef slices in a bowl and marinate them in this paste for about 1 hour. Heat the oil in a heavy frying pan or wok and fry the beef slices on both sides until lightly browned. Add the tomatoes and any marinade remaining in the bowl to the pan or wok. Stir well and gently cook the mixture until the meat is tender (about 30 minutes). Stir occasionally and add a little water now and again if it looks as though the sauce is going to dry up before the meat is cooked. The final sauce should, however, be thick.

Beef Stew in Hot Pepper Sauce (Daging Pedas)

Serves 4

This is a good recipe for cheaper cuts of meat. It is rather hot and for a milder dish you could reduce the number of chillies used.

2 tablespoons oil
1 medium onion, diced
2 cloves garlic, crushed
3–4 red chillies, fresh *or* dried, chopped *or* 1–2 teaspoons hot pepper sauce
1 teaspoon ground turmeric

1 lb (450 g) stewing beef, cubed in 1-in (2.5-cm) pieces
1 teaspoon ground cinnamon
1/2 teaspoon ground cloves
juice of 1 lemon
2 tablespoons dark soya sauce
water
salt to taste

Heat the oil in a saucepan or wok and add the onion, garlic, chillies or hot pepper sauce and turmeric. Stir fry until the onions are softened. Add the meat, cinnamon and cloves and brown the meat all over. Add the lemon juice, soya sauce and enough water to just cover the contents of the pan. Bring to the boil, reduce the heat, cover and simmer until the meat is tender (about 1 hour). Towards the end of the cooking period, remove the lid and allow the sauce to thicken. Salt to taste.

Grilled Steak Javanese Style (Bistik Daging)

Serves 4

This is really a Westernized version of a Javanese dish since an Indonesian cook would be unlikely to serve thick steaks. However, it is very good and a nice change from the usual steak dishes. Serve with fresh green salad and plain boiled rice.

1 teaspoon cumin seeds
1 tablespoon coriander seeds
2 cloves garlic, crushed
2 fl oz (50 ml) dark soya sauce
1 teaspoon brown sugar

2 tablespoons lemon *or* lime juice
salt and black pepper to taste
4 fillet steaks about 6 oz (175 g) each 1 1/2in (4 cm) thick

Crush the cumin and coriander seeds in a pestle and mortar (or use ground cumin and coriander). Put them in a small bowl and add the garlic, soya sauce, sugar and lemon or lime juice. Add salt, carefully to taste (it may not be needed since the soya sauce is already salty) and freshly ground black pepper. Put the steaks in a shallow dish and pour over the marinade. Leave them to marinate for 1–2 hours, turning once. Pre-heat the grill to high and lightly oil the grill rack. Put the steaks on the rack and grill them for 3–7 minutes (turning once during this time) depending on how well done you like your steak. If there is any marinade left, heat it and serve it in a side bowl as an accompaniment to the steaks.

Stewed Beef with Tomatoes (Daging Tomat)

Serves 4

1 lb (450 g) piece of stewing beef
water
1-in (2.5-cm) piece root ginger,
  finely chopped
juice of 1 lemon
salt to taste
3 tablespoons oil
2 fresh *or* dried red chillies,
  chopped

1 medium onion, chopped
2 cloves garlic, crushed
1 lb (450 g) tomatoes, scalded in
  boiling water, skinned and
  chopped
2 tablespoons dark soya sauce

Put the stewing beef in one piece in a pan and cover it with water. Add the ginger, lemon juice and salt to taste and bring to the boil. Cover, reduce the heat and simmer for almost 1 hour until the meat is almost tender (do not overcook). Take the meat out, allow it to cool and then cut it into 1-in (2.5-cm) cubes. Reserve the stock. Heat the oil in a frying pan or wok and fry the chillies, onion and garlic until softened. Add the cubes of meat and fry them for 3–4 minutes, stirring. Add the tomatoes, soya sauce and 8 fl oz (225 ml) of the reserved stock. Adjust the seasoning and simmer uncovered until the sauce has thickened. Serve hot.

Meatballs Javanese Style (Perkedel Daging)

Serves 4

Serve hot or cold as a side dish or in soups or, covered with tomato sauce, with rice and sambals.

1 lb (450 g) finely minced beef
1 medium onion, finely diced
2 cloves garlic, crushed
1 teaspoon hot pepper sauce
1 teaspoon ground coriander
1/2 teaspoon ground cumin
2 teaspoons dark brown sugar

2 tablespoons dark soya sauce
juice of 1 lemon
1 egg, beaten
1/2 teaspoon prawn *or* shrimp paste
  (optional)
oil for deep frying

Combine all the ingredients except the oil and mix them thoroughly by hand or in a food processor. Shape the mixture into walnut-sized balls and set them aside in a cool place for 1 hour. Heat the oil and fry the meatballs 8–10 at a time until nicely browned. Drain on absorbent paper.

CURRIED MEAT (Gulai and Kari)

Curry in various forms is popular all over Indonesia. The recipes are of Indian and/or Arabian origin and this is clearly reflected in the spices used. The many recipes followed can be approximately divided into three basic types; those that contain chillies, those that do not, and the dry fried curries devised for their keeping qualities – these are an Indonesian speciality. I have given four recipes here. The first is mild and aromatic. The second is hot and, if you are not used to hot curries, I suggest you reduce the number of chillies by half. The third is a Sumatran-style curry of medium strength and the fourth is a dry fried curry. All the curries use coconut milk. This is easily made from desiccated coconut (the method is given on page 15), or it may be bought canned from Chinese or Indian grocery stores. In Indonesia, curries are traditionally made in large quantities and then eaten throughout the week.

Note: Once coconut milk has been added to a curry, the cooking pan should be left uncovered. This prevents any chance of the coconut milk curdling and also allows water to evaporate and the sauce to thicken. Normally the curry is just ready when oil starts to separate from the sauce and to form on the surface.

Mild Lamb or Mutton Curry (Gulai Kambing)

Serves 6

2 teaspoons coriander seeds
1 teaspoon cumin seeds
5 black peppercorns
1 teaspoon ground turmeric
1-in (2.5-cm) piece root ginger, finely chopped
3 tablespoons oil
3 onions, finely sliced
4 cloves garlic, crushed

2-in (5-cm) piece cinnamon stick
3 cloves
2 cardamom pods, broken open
2 lb (1 kg) lamb *or* lean mutton cut into 1-in (2.5-cm) cubes
salt to taste
1½ pints (850 ml) fresh *or* canned coconut milk
juice of 1 lemon

Put the coriander, cumin, peppercorns, turmeric and ginger into a grinder with 1 tablespoon of oil and grind them to a smooth paste. Alternatively, prepare the paste using a pestle and mortar, adding the oil at the end. Heat the remaining oil in a heavy saucepan or wok and fry the onion and garlic in it until lightly browned. Add the spice paste, the cinnamon, cloves and cardamom and stir fry the mixture for 3–4 minutes over a moderate heat. Lift out the cinnamon and cloves.

Add the meat and stir the mixture well. Brown the meat on all sides. Add salt to taste and adjust the other seasoning if you think it's necessary. Pour in the coconut milk, stirring constantly, continue to stir and bring the curry to the boil, reduce the heat and simmer, stirring occasionally, until the meat is tender (about 45–50 minutes). Adjust the seasoning again, add the lemon juice and serve.

Variation: Add 2 medium potatoes, peeled and diced and/or 2 medium aubergines, sliced, to the curry 25 minutes before the end of the cooking time.

Chilli Hot Lamb or Mutton Curry (Gulai Jawa)

Serves 6

4 oz (100 g) desiccated coconut
2 teaspoons coriander seeds
1 teaspoon cumin seeds
1/2 teaspoon nutmeg
1 teaspoon ground turmeric
4 fresh *or* dried chillies, chopped
4 cloves garlic, crushed
1-in (2.5-cm) piece of ginger, chopped
3 tablespoons oil
2 medium onions, finely sliced

1-in (2.5-cm) piece of cinnamon stick
2 cloves
2 lb (1 kg) lean lamb *or* mutton cut into 1-in (2.5-cm) cubes
2 medium-sized ripe tomatoes, peeled and chopped
salt to taste
1 1/2 pints (750 ml) fresh *or* canned coconut milk

In a heavy frying pan or saucepan, dry fry the desiccated coconut, stirring until it is lightly browned. Set it aside. In a spice grinder or pestle and mortar grind the coriander, cumin, nutmeg, turmeric, chillies, garlic and ginger together with 1 tablespoon of oil to form a paste. If using a pestle and mortar grind the dry ingredients first, then the chillies, garlic and ginger and add the oil at the end. Heat the remaining oil in a wok or heavy pan and fry the onion until lightly browned. Add the spice paste, cinnamon stick and cloves and stir fry for 3–4 minutes. Lift out the cinnamon and cloves. Stir in the prepared desiccated coconut and then the meat. Cook and stir the mixture over a moderate heat until the meat is browned on all sides. Add the tomatoes, stir well and cook them until they are soft. Season to taste with salt. Add the coconut milk and bring the mixture slowly to the boil, stirring constantly. Reduce the heat and simmer, stirring occasionally, until the meat is tender (about 45–50 minutes).

Variation: As for mild lamb curry, see recipe above.

Curried Beef Sumatran Style (Gulai Sumatra)

Serves 4

2 teaspoons coriander seeds
1 teaspoon cumin seeds
1/2 teaspoon ground turmeric
2 cloves garlic
1 fresh *or* dried chilli *or* 1/2 teaspoon chilli powder
1/2-in (1-cm) root ginger, chopped
salt to taste
4 tablespoons oil

1 lb (450 g) stewing beef or lamb, cut into 1-in (2.5-cm) cubes
2 medium onions, diced
water *or* stock
3 medium potatoes, peeled and diced
4 fl oz (100 ml) fresh *or* canned coconut milk
1 teaspoon lemon juice

Put the coriander, cumin, turmeric, garlic, chilli, root ginger, salt and 2 tablespoons of oil into a grinder and blend the mixture to a paste. Alternatively, use a pestle and mortar. Put the meat in a bowl with the spice paste and coat each cube of meat with paste. Heat the remaining oil in a wok or pan and stir fry the onions until softened. Add the meat cubes and paste and stir fry gently until the meat cubes are browned on all sides. Just cover the meat with water or stock, bring it to the boil, reduce the heat, cover and simmer until the meat is half done (about 20 minutes). Add the potatoes and recover the pan and continue cooking until they and the meat are tender (about another 25 minutes). Remove the pan lid to thicken up the sauce about 15 minutes after adding the potatoes. Add the coconut milk, stir well and continue to simmer the mixture for a further 5 minutes. The sauce should be thick and creamy. Add the lemon juice and serve.

Sumatran Style Curried Lamb Chops (Kari Kambing Padang)

Serves 4

2 tablespoons oil
1 small onion, finely diced
2 cloves garlic, crushed
1/2 chilli pepper, finely chopped *or* 1/4 teaspoon hot pepper sauce
4 macadamia nuts *or* almonds *or* brazil nuts
1/2 teaspoon ground turmeric
1/2 teaspoon ground ginger
salt and pepper to taste

1 teaspoon grated lemon rind *or* lemon grass
4 lean lamb chops
juice of 1 lemon
1 teaspoon dark brown sugar
1 teaspoon ground coriander
8 fl oz (225 ml) water
8 fl oz (225 ml) coconut milk fresh *or* canned

Put the oil, onion, garlic, chilli or hot pepper sauce, nuts, turmeric, ginger powder, salt, pepper and lemon rind or lemon grass into a blender and blend the mixture to a paste or, alternatively, make the paste by hand using a pestle and mortar. Fry the paste in a wok or heavy frying pan, stirring constantly for 1 or 2 minutes. Add the chops and fry them on both sides until browned. Add the lemon juice, sugar, coriander and water, mix well, cover and gently simmer until the chops are almost tender (about 20 minutes). Stir in the coconut milk and bring the pan slowly to a gentle boil. Adjust the seasoning and simmer for 5 minutes. Serve.

Dry Fried Curried Meat (Rendang Daging)

Serves 8

Because this dish takes quite a long time to prepare, keeps very well and improves with age, it is normally made in large quantities. The unused curry will keep for up to a week in the fridge or for much longer in a deep freeze. The curry is cooked slowly until all the water has evaporated. A residue of oil is left behind and in the final stage of the cooking process, the meat fries in the oil and all the flavour is sealed in.

1 medium onion, chopped
1-in (2.5-cm) piece root ginger, chopped
3 cloves garlic
4 chillies, chopped *or* 2 teaspoons hot pepper sauce
4 macadamia nuts *or* almonds *or* brazil nuts
1 teaspoon ground turmeric
1 teaspoon ground coriander

½ teaspoon ground cumin
2 pints (1 litre) fresh *or* canned coconut milk
2 teaspoons finely chopped lemon rind *or* lemon leaves
2 bay leaves *or* daun salem leaves
salt to taste
3 lb (1.5 kg) lean beef or mutton, cut in 2-in (5-cm) cubes

Put the onion, ginger, garlic, chillies or hot pepper sauce, nuts, turmeric, coriander and cumin powder into a blender, switch on and then add enough coconut milk to form the mixture into a smooth thin paste. Put this paste and all the remaining ingredients except the meat into a thick-bottomed saucepan. Stir well and bring the mixture gently to a slow boil, stirring continuously. Add the meat, return to the boil, stirring all the time. Reduce the heat to very low and simmer, uncovered, stirring often, until the meat is tender. This will take about 2 hours. By the time the meat is tender the oil in the mixture will have separated from the other ingredients. Stir it back in and carry on cooking and stirring for another 30 minutes, or until the meat has turned a dark brown and has absorbed nearly all the sauce. Serve immediately or allow to cool and store until required.

Variation 1: In some recipes, although I have not tried them, the onion, ginger, garlic, chillies, nuts, turmeric, coriander and cumin powder are fried in oil before being blended to a paste with the coconut milk. This may give the dish a slightly different flavour.

Variation 2: Follow the recipe for dry fried meat curry above but reduce the quantity of ingredients by half. Stop cooking the dish at the point where the meat is tender. This dish is delicious but doesn't keep as well as the dry fried version which is why I recommend you only to make half the amount.

Lace Pancakes to accompany Curry (Roti Jala)

Roti jala pancakes are made by dropping the pancake batter on to a hot plate or frying pan through a perforated ladle or from your finger tips. In each case the aim is to form a pancake with a lace pattern. The pancake is cooked until just set but not browned and is served hot with curries.

10 oz (275 g) sifted white flour	1 pint (550 ml) water, milk *or* fresh
2 eggs	*or* canned coconut milk
salt to taste	oil for frying

In a bowl or food processor, combine the flour, eggs, salt and water or coconut milk and beat them into a smooth, thin batter. Lightly oil a frying pan, dip your fingers in the batter and allow it to run into the frying pan as you move your hand round the pan. Alternatively, pour a small amount of the batter through a perforated ladle with large holes and move the ladle round the pan. Gently cook the pancake until it sets and then turn it over. Repeat on the other side and remove the roti jala from the pan before it is browned. Repeat for all the batter. Store the roti in a warm oven and serve as soon as possible.

Fried Spiced Pork in Soya Sauce (Babi Kecap)

Serves 4

2 tablespoons oil	2 teaspoons dark brown sugar
1 small onion, finely chopped	1/2 teaspoon nutmeg
2 cloves garlic, crushed	1 clove
1 lb (450 g) lean pork cut into 1-in (2.5-cm) cubes	pepper to taste
	water *or* stock
3 tablespoons dark soya sauce	

Heat the oil in a pan and fry the onion and garlic until lightly coloured. Add the pork and fry, stirring, over a medium heat for 4–5 minutes. Turn the heat down and add the soya sauce, sugar, nutmeg, clove and pepper to taste. Stir well and cook for 2 minutes. Add enough water or stock to just cover the pork and bring the mixture to the boil. Reduce the heat and simmer, uncovered, for 30 minutes or until the pork is just tender and the sauce is thick.

Chilli Hot Marinated Pork in Coconut Milk (Sambal Goreng Babi)

Serves 4

Reduce the number of chillies if you wish to reduce the fierceness of this dish, otherwise have plenty of cucumber slices available for cooling hot mouths.

1 lb (450 g) pork cut into 1-in (2.5-cm) cubes
4–6 red fresh *or* dried chillies, finely chopped
3 cloves garlic, crushed
1/2-in (1-cm) piece of root ginger, finely chopped
2 teaspoons brown sugar
1 teaspoon prawn paste (optional)

1 teaspoon salt
2 tablespoons oil
1 medium onion, diced
1 teaspoon grated lemon peel *or* lemon grass
juice of 1 lemon
16 fl oz (450 ml) fresh *or* canned coconut milk

Put the pork in a bowl and stir in the chillies, garlic, ginger, sugar, prawn paste (if used) and salt. Leave to marinate for 30 minutes. Heat the oil in a wok or saucepan and fry the onion until lightly coloured. Add the pork and marinade and stir fry the mixture over a medium heat for 2–3 minutes. Add the lemon peel or lemon grass, lemon juice and coconut milk. Mix well and bring to a gentle simmer. Cook until the pork is tender and the sauce has thickened (about 40 minutes).

Fried Spiced Pork Meatballs (Perkedel Babi Goreng)

Serves 4

These can be served on their own, hot, as a savoury dish with drinks or as a main meal with boiled rice and sambals and other dishes.

1 lb (450 g) slightly fatty pork, minced
1 medium onion, finely diced
2 cloves garlic, crushed
1 teaspoon ground coriander
1 tablespoon dark soya sauce
1 teaspoon brown sugar
salt and pepper to taste
2 eggs, beaten
oil for deep frying

Combine all the ingredients, except the eggs and oil, in a bowl. Stir the mixture well and then break in the eggs. Beat this mixture to a smooth consistency and then shape it into small balls about 1 in (2.5 cm) in diameter. Deep fry batches of the balls in hot oil until nicely browned. Drain and serve.

Balinese Fried Liver (Hati Goreng Bali)

Serves 4

2 cloves garlic, crushed
1 teaspoon ground turmeric
1 chilli, finely chopped *or* 1/2 teaspoon hot pepper sauce
1 tablespoon crunchy peanut butter
1 lb (450 g) calf's or lamb's liver, in 1/2-in (1-cm) slices
salt and pepper to taste
2 tablespoons oil
1 medium onion, finely diced
2 cloves garlic, crushed
8 fl oz (225 ml) coconut milk fresh *or* canned
juice of 1/2 lemon

Put the garlic, turmeric, chilli and peanut butter into a bowl and mix well. Stir the liver slices into the bowl and add salt and pepper to taste. Heat the oil in a wok or frying pan and stir fry the onion and garlic until lightly coloured. Add the liver mixture and brown the liver slices on both sides. Reduce the heat and add the coconut milk. Bring to a gentle boil and cook, stirring, for 7–8 minutes or until the liver is tender and the sauce has thickened. Add the lemon juice and the dish is ready to serve.

MEAT KEBABS (Sate)

Sate is a favourite Indonesian food and there are sate stalls in villages and cities all over the country. Sate is basically skewers of meat (in Indonesia the skewers are made of bamboo) which are grilled over hot coals, and then dipped in a sauce before serving. The sauces are usually peanut based and range from mild to very hot. Sometimes the meat is marinated before being grilled and is brushed with the marinade during grilling. Lean lamb, mutton, chicken, beef and pork are all used for making sate.

In the recipes below I have given directions for making a variety of sate sauces and marinades followed by two general recipes, one for preparing sate without a marinade and one for preparing it with a marinade. Thus you select a meat, a sate sauce and, if you wish, a marinade as well and proceed accordingly. Further marinades are given with the Chicken Sate recipe (see page 99).

At the end of the section there is a recipe for spiced sate (Sate Bumbu). This is different from the normal sate in that it is served without a sauce. Sate dishes are really delicious, popular with most people and easy to prepare.

Prawn Sate (Sate Udang)

Note: In any of the following recipes prawns, shelled and deveined, could be substituted for the meat. Thread about 4 prawns onto each stick or skewer before grilling.

Meat Sate

Method 1: without marinade

Serves 4

1 lb (450 g) lean lamb, mutton,   sate sauce (see recipes below)
  beef, pork *or* chicken

Make the sate sauce. Cut the meat into 1/2-in (1-cm) cubes and thread the cubes onto skewers (bamboo if possible), leaving a small space between each cube and a space at each end so they can be held easily. Grill the meat over glowing coals or under a hot grill, rotating frequently until nicely browned on all sides. Serve the sate on skewers in a serving dish with the sate sauce poured over them. Alternatively, serve the sate on separate plates with individual bowls of sauce to accompany them.

Note: If you are using bamboo skewers with a domestic grill and you find that the ends start to smoulder during grilling, cover them with a twist of kitchen foil. Take this foil off before serving.

Method 2: with marinade

Serves 4

sate sauce (see recipes below)   1 lb (450 g) lamb *or* mutton *or* beef
marinade (see recipes below)   *or* pork *or* chicken

Choose and make a marinade and a sauce from the recipes given below. Cut the meat into 1/2-in (1-cm) cubes and stir them in a bowl of the selected marinade. Make sure each cube is well-coated. Set the meat aside to marinate for at least 1 hour. Now thread the marinated cubes on to the skewers (bamboo if possible) leaving a small space between each cube of meat and a space at each end of the skewer so they can be held easily. Cook the sate over glowing coals or under a very hot grill, rotating frequently until the meat is nicely browned on all sides. Brush them with the marinade during grilling. Serve the sate on skewers in a serving dish with a sauce poured over them and accompanied by the remaining marinade in a side dish. Alternatively, serve the sate on individual plates with individual bowls of sauce and a communal dish of marinade.

Mild Peanut Sauce (Bumbu Kacang)

1 tablespoon oil
1 small onion, finely diced
1/4 teaspoon chilli powder *or* hot pepper sauce
8 fl oz (225 ml) water

8 oz (225 g) peanuts fried in 1 tablespoon oil and crushed *or* 8 oz (225 g) crunchy peanut butter
1 teaspoon dark brown sugar
juice of 1/2 lemon
1 tablespoon dark soya sauce
salt to taste

Heat the oil in a saucepan and add the onion. Sauté until the onion is lightly coloured. Add the chilli powder or hot pepper sauce, water, crushed peanuts or peanut butter and sugar and stir well. Bring the mixture to a gentle boil and continue cooking and stirring until the sauce is smooth and thick. Stir in the lemon juice and soya sauce. Add salt to taste if necessary.

Variation: This sauce can be made spicy hot by sautéeing 1 or 2 finely chopped chilli peppers with the onion.

Chilli Hot Peanut Sauce (Bumbu Kacang Pedas)

2 tablespoons oil
2-4 fresh *or* dried chilli peppers, finely diced
2 cloves garlic, crushed
1 small onion, finely diced
1 1/2 teaspoons curry powder

8 oz (225 g) peanuts fried in 1 tablespoon oil and crushed *or* 8 oz (225 g) crunchy peanut butter
8 fl oz (225 ml) water
1 tablespoon brown sugar
1 teaspoon grated lemon peel *or* chopped lemon grass
salt and pepper to taste

Heat the oil in a saucepan and add the chillies, garlic, onion and curry powder and sauté the mixture until the onion is just browned. Add the remaining ingredients, stir well and bring to a gentle boil. Reduce the heat and cook, stirring until the sauce is thick, and smooth. (For quick peanut sauce recipe see page 50).

Special Soya Sauce (Bumbu Jawa)

1 small onion, finely diced
4 tablespoons dark soya sauce
juice of 1 lemon

3/4 teaspoon chilli powder *or* hot pepper sauce
pepper to taste

Put all the ingredients into a small bowl and mix well. It is now ready to serve.

Soya Sauce Marinade (Bumbu Kecap)

1 small onion, finely diced
3 tablespoons dark soya sauce

1 teaspoon dark brown sugar
pepper to taste

Combine all the ingredients and mix well. The marinade is now ready.

Sweet and Sour Marinade (Bumbu Asam Manis)

1 small onion, finely diced
2 cloves garlic, crushed
3 tablespoons dark soya sauce
1 teaspoon ground ginger
1/2 teaspoon ground coriander

2 tablespoons tamarind water *or* 2 tablespoons lemon juice
2 teaspoons dark brown sugar
pepper to taste

Combine all the ingredients and mix well. The marinade is now ready.

Chilli Hot Marinade (Bumbu Pedas)

1 medium onion, chopped
1-in (2.5-cm) piece of root ginger, chopped
2 red fresh *or* dried chillies

1 tablespoon lemon juice
2 tablespoons dark soya sauce
1 tablespoon dark brown sugar
1 tablespoon oil

Put all the ingredients into a blender and blend them to a smooth paste. The marinade is now ready.

Coconut Marinade (Bumbu Kelapa)

Prepare one of the above marinades and simply stir into it 2 tablespoons of desiccated coconut moistened with 1 tablespoon hot water.

Shrimp or Prawn Paste Marinade (Bumbu Terasi)

Prepare one of the above marinades and stir into it 1 teaspoon of prawn or shrimp paste (terasi).

Spiced Sate (Sate Daging Bumbu)

Serves 4

Serve very hot with boiled rice.

1 lb (450 g) lean meat (beef is usually used but other meat is suitable)
1 small onion, chopped
2 cloves garlic, crushed
2 red chilli peppers, fresh *or* dried
1-in (2.5-cm) piece root ginger, chopped
2 tablespoons oil
1 teaspoon coriander seeds, crushed
1/2 teaspoon ground turmeric
1 teaspoon brown sugar
2 teaspoons grated lemon rind *or* chopped lemon grass
4 fl oz (100 ml) water *or* coconut milk, fresh *or* canned

Cut the meat into 1/2-in (1-cm) cubes. Put the onion, garlic, chillies, ginger and half the oil into a blender and blend them to a smooth paste. Heat the remaining oil in a wok or frying pan and add the paste, coriander, turmeric, sugar and lemon rind or lemon grass and stir fry for 2–3 minutes. Add the meat and stir fry until just browned. Add the water or coconut milk and reduce the heat to a simmer. Cook and stir until the sauce is almost dry. Remove the meat cubes from the pan and thread them onto skewers (bamboo if possible), leaving a small space between each cube of meat and one at each end so they can be held easily. Cook the sate over glowing coals or under a hot grill, rotating frequently, until nicely browned. Brush during grilling with any sauce left in the frying pan.

CHICKEN DISHES
(Masakan Ayam)

Chicken is most popular in Indonesia and is cooked in a number of interesting ways. The most common cooking techniques used are frying, grilling over hot charcoal (a domestic oven grill is a good substitute and can be used for all the recipes given here that require grilling) and braising in water or coconut milk. However, many chicken recipes include a combination of or all of these methods as well as a stage at which the chicken is marinated.

Ovens are uncommon in Indonesia and, consequently, there are not many recipes for roast chicken. However, I have included some roast chicken recipes here which are adaptations of more traditionally cooked dishes.

A number of the chicken recipes use coconut milk but I hope that if you're unfamiliar with this ingredient this won't put you off from trying them. Coconut milk can be easily made from desiccated coconut (see page 15) and it can also be bought canned from Chinese grocery stores.

For instructions on how to cut a chicken into serving pieces see Cook's Notes.

Chicken in Marinade, Grilled (Ayam Panggang)

Serves 6

The chicken is cut into serving pieces (or you could use chicken legs or breasts) and marinated before grilling or barbecuing. I have given two marinades; one is soya sauce based and the other is a hot chilli based marinade. If you are not used to very hot food you may wish to modify the chilli based marinade by reducing the number of chillies in it. Serve the chicken with boiled rice, sambals and a salad.

2–3 lb (1–1.5 kg) roasting *or* spring
   chicken cut into serving pieces
   or the same weight of chicken
   portions

Marinade 1: with soya sauce

4 tablespoons dark soya sauce
3 tablespoons oil
juice of 1 lemon

2 cloves garlic, crushed
black pepper to taste

Marinade 2: with chilli

3 tablespoons oil
6 chillies, fresh *or* dried, finely
   chopped, *or* 3 teaspoons hot
   pepper sauce
2 cloves garlic, crushed
1 small onion, grated

juice of 1 lemon
1 tablespoon dark soya sauce
1 teaspoon dark brown sugar
1/2 teaspoon ground coriander
1 teaspoon pepper
salt to taste

Select the marinade you wish to prepare and combine the ingredients in a bowl. Put the chicken pieces in the bowl, coat with the marinade and leave to marinate for 1 hour. Preheat a moderately hot grill or prepare a barbecue fire and have the charcoal glowing. Place the chicken pieces on a tray under the grill or on skewers over the charcoal and cook them on both sides, basting regularly with the marinade until the chicken is nicely browned and tender. Ideally, the chicken should be cooked inside before the outside is over browned. To check that the chicken is cooked, push a skewer into it and when the juices run clear and are no longer bloody the chicken is done.

Variation: To serve this dish in the traditional manner prepare the chicken by splitting it in half down the back. Marinate it and cook it in 2 pieces.

Roasted Chicken in Marinade, Grilled (Ayam Panggang Kecap)

Serves 6

This recipe is the same as the one above except that the chicken is partially roasted before being marinated and grilled. This method produces a very tasty, slightly crisp chicken. Thus, wash and dry inside and out a roasting or spring chicken weighing 2–3 lb (1–1.5 kg). Lightly season it with salt and pepper and roast in a preheated oven 375° F (190° C, gas mark 5) for 30 minutes. Take it out of the oven and allow it to cool enough so that you can touch it. Cut the chicken into 4 or more pieces and then follow the recipe above for chicken in marinade, grilled.

Chicken with Coconut Sauce, Grilled or Roasted (Ayam Panggang Bumbu Besengek)

Serves 6

There are two methods for preparing this dish. In the first the whole chicken is rubbed with spices and then roasted in coconut milk. In the second the chicken is cut into pieces and fried in spices, then boiled in coconut milk and finally grilled.

2–3 lb (1–1.5 kg) roasting *or* spring chicken, washed inside and out, dried
2 tablespoons oil
2 medium onions, grated
2 cloves garlic, crushed
1 teaspoon grated lemon rind *or* chopped lemon grass

1 teaspoon ground coriander
1/2 teaspoon ground cumin
1 teaspoon ground turmeric
1 teaspoon chilli powder
1 teaspoon salt
1 pint (550 ml) fresh *or* canned coconut milk

Combine the onion, garlic, lemon rind or lemon grass, coriander, cumin, turmeric, chilli, a little coconut milk and salt and blend the mixture to a smooth paste in an electric blender or pound with a pestle and mortar.

Method 1

Preheat the oven to 375° F (190° C, gas mark 5). Heat the oil in a wok or small frying pan. Stir in the prepared spice paste and cook it, stirring, for about 2 minutes or until fragrant, over a moderate heat. Allow the paste to cool and then brush it over the chicken inside and out. Stir any left-over paste into the coconut milk. Put the chicken in a roasting dish. Bring the coconut milk to a gentle boil and then simmer it, uncovered, for 5 minutes. Pour the coconut milk over the chicken and then place in the preheated oven. Roast the chicken for about 1 hour, or until the chicken is golden brown and tender, basting occasionally. Transfer the chicken to a serving dish and serve the liquid from the roasting pan in a separate bowl.

Method 2

Cut the chicken into serving pieces. Heat the oil in a wok or frying pan, stir in the prepared spice paste and cook it, stirring, for 1 or 2 minutes over a moderate heat. Add the chicken pieces and brown them on both sides. Gently pour in the coconut milk and cook the dish over a low heat for 30 minutes, stirring occasionally. Remove the chicken pieces from the frying pan, place them on a wire grill tray, brush them with a little oil and grill or barbecue them on both sides until nicely browned. Meanwhile, keep the coconut sauce simmering. Finally, adjust the seasoning of the sauce and serve it in a separate bowl with the grilled chicken.

Spiced Grilled Chicken (Singgang Ayam)

Serves 6

For this recipe the chicken is traditionally chopped down the breast-bone and trussed into a spread-eagled position. It is then cooked in this shape. However, most people do not have a pan large enough to use this method so I suggest halving or quartering the chicken for easier management. The chicken is marinated, braised in coconut milk and then browned under the grill or in the oven.

2–3 lb (1–1.5 kg) roasting *or* spring
  chicken, halved or quartered
2 medium onions, grated
4 cloves garlic, crushed
2 fresh *or* dried red chillies *or* 1
  teaspoon hot pepper sauce
1-in (2.5-cm) piece of root ginger,
  chopped
1 teaspoon ground turmeric

1 teaspoon ground coriander
1 teaspoon pepper
1 teaspoon salt
1 pint (550 ml) fresh *or* canned
  coconut milk
2 bay leaves *or* daun salem leaves
1 tablespoon lemon juice *or*
  tamarind water

Put the onion, garlic, chillies or hot pepper sauce, ginger, turmeric, coriander, pepper and salt into a blender and blend them to a paste, or use a pestle and mortar. Rub the chicken pieces all over with the paste and set them aside for 1 hour. Put the coconut milk, bay leaves and lemon juice into a large pan and bring them slowly to the boil. Put in the chicken pieces and simmer for 50 minutes until the chicken is tender. During this time occasionally ladle the cooking liquid over the chicken and turn the pieces over. Lift the chicken out and leave the sauce simmering. Gently brown the chicken pieces on both sides under a grill, over a charcoal fire or in a preheated oven 375° F (190° C, gas mark 5). Serve the chicken with the coconut sauce in a separate bowl.

White Curried Chicken (Opor Ayam)

Serves 6

This is a mild dish, pale in colour and very suitable for people who do not like hot curries. If you wish to pep it up, serve a hot sambal side dish.

1 teaspoon ground coriander	1 teaspoon grated lemon rind *or* 1
1 teaspoon ground cumin	stalk lemon grass
1/4 teaspoon ground cloves	2–3 lb (1–1.5 kg) chicken cut into
1/2 teaspoon ground turmeric	serving pieces *or* the same
1/4 teaspoon chilli powder	weight of chicken pieces
3 tablespoons oil	2 bay leaves *or* daun salem leaves
4 cloves garlic, crushed	16 fl oz (450 ml) fresh *or* canned
1-in (2.5-cm) piece root ginger,	coconut milk
finely chopped (optional)	1 tablespoon lemon juice
2 medium onions, finely sliced	salt to taste

Combine the coriander, cumin, cloves, turmeric and chilli powder in a bowl and stir the mixture to a paste with a little of the oil. Heat the remaining oil in a heavy frying pan or wok and fry the onion, garlic and ginger (if used) until the onion is softened. Put in the spice paste and chicken pieces and stir them together over the heat until the chicken pieces are coloured by the spices. Add the lemon rind or lemon grass, bay leaves or daun salem leaves and coconut milk and bring the mixture to a gentle boil, reduce the heat and simmer for 50 minutes or until the chicken is tender and the sauce is thick. Stir in the lemon juice and add salt to taste.

Variation: When the chicken is half cooked add 8 oz (225 g) of fresh or tinned pineapple pieces to the pan.

Hot Javanese Curried Chicken (Gulai Ayam)

Serves 6

Javanese curry is given its distinctive taste by the addition of grated or desiccated coconut dry fried and then crushed into a paste.

2 tablespoons oil
2 medium onions, finely chopped
6 cloves garlic, crushed
1-in (2.5-cm) piece root ginger, chopped
4 fresh *or* dried red chillies *or* 2 teaspoons chilli powder (use less for a milder dish)
4 almonds *or* macadamia nuts
1 teaspoon ground coriander
1/2 teaspoon ground turmeric
1 teaspoon grated lemon rind *or* 1 stalk lemon grass

2 whole cloves
1-in (2.5-cm) piece cinnamon bark (optional)
2–3 lb (1–1.5 kg) chicken cut into serving pieces *or* the same weight of chicken portions
1 pint (550 ml) coconut milk, fresh *or* canned
2 oz (50 g) desiccated or freshly grated coconut
1 tablespoon lemon *or* lime juice
salt to taste

Heat the oil in a heavy pan, frying pan or wok and stir fry the onion until softened. Put the garlic, ginger, chillies, nuts, coriander, turmeric and 3 tablespoons of the coconut milk into a food blender and blend them to a paste, or use a pestle and mortar. Add this paste, the lemon rind or lemon grass, the cloves and cinnamon bark (if used) to the frying pan and stir fry the mixture for 1–2 minutes. Add the chicken pieces and coat them with the spice mixture. Stir in the coconut milk and bring everything to a gentle boil, reduce the heat and set the pan to a very low simmer. Cook very gently for 50 minutes, or until the chicken is tender. Meanwhile, in another frying pan, brown the desiccated coconut over a low heat, without any oil, and stir it. Remove the coconut from the pan, and grind it to a paste in a pestle and mortar or use the back of a wooden spoon. Stir this paste into the chicken halfway through the cooking period. When the chicken is tender add the lemon or lime juice and season to taste with salt.

Boiled Chicken in Coconut Milk (Ayam Santan)

Serves 6

This chicken dish is simple to make and delicious. It is essentially only chicken boiled in spiced coconut milk.

1 medium onion, grated
2 cloves garlic, crushed
4 almonds *or* macadamia nuts
1 teaspoon coriander seeds
1/2 teaspoon cumin seeds
1 teaspoon hot pepper sauce
1 teaspoon ground ginger
1/2 teaspoon turmeric
1 1/4 pints (700 ml) coconut milk,
   fresh *or* canned

1 bay leaf *or* daun salem leaf
1 teaspoon grated lemon rind *or* 1
   stalk lemon grass
salt to taste
2–3 lb (1–1.5 kg) chicken cut into
   serving pieces *or* the same
   weight of chicken portions

Combine the onion, garlic, nuts, coriander, cumin, hot pepper sauce, ginger and turmeric in a blender and blend them to a paste, or use a pestle and mortar. Put the coconut milk into a large pan and add the paste to it (if using a blender, clean it out with some of the coconut milk). Add the bay leaf or daun salem leaf, lemon rind or lemon grass and salt to taste. Bring the mixture slowly to a very gentle boil, stirring, and then add the chicken pieces. Return the pan to the boil, reduce the heat and simmer the chicken uncovered until it is tender (about 50 minutes). Adjust the seasoning and serve.

Chicken Sate (Sate Ayam)

Serves 6

Chicken pieces are marinated, threaded on skewers and grilled. Chicken sate is popular and versatile. Serve it as a snack, a starter, as part of a barbecue or as a main course with rice. For more information on sate and sate sauces see pages 88–92.

4 chicken breasts, skinned, boned,
   cut into 1/2-in (1-cm) cubes plus
   one of the following marinades

Marinade 1: soya sauce and lemon

3 tablespoons dark soya sauce
1 teaspoon dark brown sugar
1 small onion, finely diced

2 tablespoons lemon juice
1/4 teaspoon chilli powder
   (optional)

Combine the ingredients and mix them well. The marinade is ready to use immediately.

Marinade 2: coconut and peanuts

2 tablespoons oil
1 small onion, finely diced
1 clove garlic, crushed
1 teaspoon coriander seeds,
  crushed
1 tablespoon crunchy peanut butter

1/4 teaspoon chilli powder
  (optional)
2 tablespoons desiccated coconut
  (quickly dry fried until just
  browned)

Heat the oil in a small pan and add the onion, garlic, coriander seeds, peanut butter and chilli powder. Stir over a low heat for 2 minutes. Remove from the heat and stir in the coconut. Thread the chicken cubes onto skewers (bamboo are best). Place the chosen marinade on a plate and coat the skewered chicken cubes with it and then grill them over glowing charcoal or under a hot grill, turning frequently, for 5 minutes or until nicely browned. During this time, brush the chicken cubes occasionally with any remaining marinade. Serve the sate on the skewers with rice.

Chicken Sate with Peanut Sauce

Serves 6

Serve the chicken sate as prepared above with one of the peanut sauces given in the sate recipes on page 90.

Fried Chicken (Ayam Goreng)

Serves 6

This is the Javanese way of frying chicken. The method, which involves boiling the chicken in water or coconut milk before frying, produces tender and crisp pieces of tasty chicken.

2–3 lb (1–1.5 kg) spring chicken
  cut into serving pieces *or* the
  same weight of chicken portions
1 1/4 pints (700 ml) water *or* fresh *or*
  canned coconut milk
1 medium onion, finely chopped
1 fresh *or* dried red chilli, chopped
  or 1/2 teaspoon chilli powder
1/2 teaspoon ground turmeric

1 teaspoon coriander seeds, lightly
  crushed
1/2 teaspoon cumin seeds, crushed
1 bay leaf *or* daun salem leaf
1 teaspoon grated lemon rind *or* 1
  stalk lemon grass, chopped
salt to taste
oil for frying

Put all the ingredients into a large pan, except the oil, and bring them to the boil. Reduce the heat, cover the pan (unless you are using coconut milk) and simmer slowly for 50 minutes to 1 hour, or until the chicken is tender. Remove the chicken pieces from the pan and drain them off. Reserve the contents of the pan to serve with the chicken. Heat the oil and shallow or deep fry the chicken pieces on both sides until golden brown. Drain the chicken on absorbent kitchen paper and serve it with the hot cooking liquor in a separate bowl.

Fried Chicken Padang Style (Ayam Goreng Padang)

Serves 6

Padang in Sumatra is well known in Indonesia for its superb cuisine and this recipe, although a little complicated, does Padang cooking justice. It is similar to the fried chicken recipe above but has one more stage.

The ingredients are as for the fried chicken recipe above, but use only 8 fl oz (225 ml) water or coconut milk. Put the onion, chilli, turmeric, coriander, cumin and 3 tablespoons of the water or coconut milk into the container of a food blender and blend the mixture to a smooth paste, or use a pestle and mortar. Brush the chicken pieces with this paste and leave them to marinate for 1 hour. Put the coated chicken pieces in a pan with the water or coconut milk. Bring the pan to the boil, reduce the heat, cover (unless you are using coconut milk) and simmer the chicken for 50 minutes to 1 hour or until it is tender. Remove the chicken pieces from the pan and drain them off. Reserve the contents of the pan to serve with the chicken. Heat the oil and shallow or deep fry the chicken pieces on both sides until golden brown. Drain the chicken on absorbent kitchen paper and serve it with the hot cooking liquor in a separate bowl.

Fried Chicken with Rice (Nasi Ayam Goreng)

Serves 6–8

Serve this dish with a selection of sambals.

1 lb (450 g) long grain rice, washed and drained
2 lb (1 kg) chicken portions
1 medium onion, finely diced
2 cloves garlic, crushed
1-in (2.5-cm) piece root ginger, finely chopped *or* ½ teaspoon ground ginger

2 teaspoons crushed coriander seeds
1 teaspoon crushed cumin seeds
1-in (2.5-cm) piece cinnamon stick
1 teaspoon grated lemon peel
salt and black pepper to taste
oil for shallow frying

To garnish
chopped celery tops
cucumber, peeled, deseeded, diced

Cover the rice with water and set it aside. Put the chicken pieces and the remaining ingredients, except the oil, in a pot and just cover them with water. Bring the chicken to the boil, reduce the heat and gently boil 'until the chicken is just tender (about 40 minutes). Lift out the chicken pieces and set them aside. Reserve the stock in a separate bowl. Drain off the rice. Heat 2 tablespoons of oil in a heavy saucepan and stir fry the rice for 3–4 minutes. Add 1 pint (550 ml) of the reserved stock (make up the amount with water if there is not enough stock) and bring it to the boil. Cover the pan with a tightly fitting lid (wrap the lid in aluminium foil to improve the fit if necessary), reduce the heat to very low and simmer the rice for 20 minutes. Before the rice is cooked heat the oil in a frying pan or wok and shallow fry the chicken pieces on both sides until golden brown. Transfer the rice to a serving dish and shape it into a mound. Surround the rice with fried chicken pieces and garnish the peak with chopped celery tops and diced cucumber.

Fried Chicken and Chillied Tomatoes (Ayam Tomat Lombok)

Serves 6

This dish only works well with young, tender pieces of chicken. It is very hot and should be approached with caution if you are unused to chillies.

2–3 lb (1–1.5 kg) spring chicken
    cut into serving pieces *or* the
    same weight of chicken portions
oil for frying
1 medium onion, finely chopped
3–6 fresh *or* dried red chillies,
    finely chopped

juice of 1 lemon
8 oz (225 g) fresh tomatoes, peeled
    and chopped *or* tinned tomatoes,
    chopped
salt to taste

Heat the oil and deep or shallow fry the chicken pieces until nicely browned and just tender. Drain and set them aside. Put a little oil in a wok or frying pan and stir fry the onion and chillies over a moderate heat until the onion is softened. Add the lemon juice, tomatoes and salt to taste and cook until the tomatoes are very soft. Put in the fried chicken pieces, mix well and stir over a medium flame until the chicken is well heated through. Serve.

Fried Chicken in Soya Sauce (Ayam Goreng Kecap)

Serves 6

2–3 lb (1–1.5 kg) spring chicken
   cut into serving pieces *or* the
   same weight of chicken portions
water
oil for shallow frying
1 small onion, finely chopped
2 cloves garlic, crushed

1–2 fresh *or* dried red chillies,
   finely chopped
3 tablespoons dark soya sauce
juice of 1 lemon
1 tablespoon tomato purée
salt and pepper to taste

Put the chicken pieces in a pan and cover them with water. Bring them to the boil and cook over a medium heat for 20 minutes. Remove the chicken pieces from the pot and drain them, reserving the chicken stock. Heat the oil in a frying pan or wok and shallow fry the chicken pieces on both sides until browned. Remove them from the pan and drain. Add the onion, garlic and chillies to the frying pan. Stir fry them until the onion is softened. Return the chicken to the pan, add the soya sauce, lemon juice, tomato purée and salt and pepper to taste. Add 4 fl oz (100 ml) of the chicken stock, mix it well in and leave to simmer for 10 minutes or until the chicken is tender and the sauce is thick.

Chicken in Lemon or Tamarind Marinade, Fried (Ayam Goreng Asam Garam)

Serves 6

A simple but effective recipe. Chicken cooked like this is good on its own as a light meal or as part of a buffet. For a traditional Indonesian flavour, tamarind water and not lemon juice should be used.

2–3 lb (1–1.5 kg) spring chicken
   cut into serving pieces *or* the
   same weight of chicken portions
oil for deep or shallow frying

Marinade

1 tablespoon vegetable oil
4 fl oz (100 ml) lemon juice *or*
   tamarind water
2 cloves garlic, crushed
1/2 teaspoon ground ginger
1 teaspoon ground coriander
1 teaspoon salt

Combine the marinade ingredients in a bowl and put in the chicken pieces. Brush them with the marinade and leave them to marinate for 2 hours. Remove the chicken pieces and drain them. Heat the oil and deep fry the chicken pieces until they are golden brown on both sides. Alternatively, shallow fry them, covered, giving each side about 6 minutes, until they are golden brown and tender.

Quick Fried Chicken (Ayam Goreng Bumbu)

Serves 6

Use very young and tender pieces of chicken for this dish.

1 spring chicken cut into serving
    pieces *or* a suitable number of
    chicken legs and breasts
lemon juice
salt and pepper to taste
ground coriander to taste

ground cumin to taste
oil for deep frying

To garnish
2 lemons, cut into wedges

Sprinkle the chicken pieces with lemon juice, salt, pepper, coriander and cumin to taste. Heat the oil to about 350° F (180° C) and deep fry the chicken pieces until golden brown. Serve garnished with lemon wedges.

Fried Chicken Balinese Style (Ayam Goreng Bali)

Serves 6

In this recipe the chicken is fried in a spicy paste until half cooked, then water or coconut milk is added and the chicken is simmered until tender. The result is a very tender, spicy chicken dish with a slightly crisp texture.

2 tablespoons oil
2–3 lb (1–1.5 kg) spring chicken
    cut into serving pieces *or* the
    same weight of chicken portions
1 medium onion, chopped
2 fresh *or* dried red chillies
    (optional)
2 cloves garlic, crushed
1-in (2.5-cm) piece of root ginger,
    chopped

5 almonds *or* macadamia nuts
1 tablespoon dark soya sauce
1 teaspoon ground coriander
1/2 teaspoon ground cumin
1/2 teaspoon ground turmeric
8 fl oz (225 ml) water *or* fresh *or*
    canned coconut milk
1 tablespoon white vinegar
2 teaspoons dark brown sugar
salt to taste

Heat the oil in a wok or frying pan and fry the chicken pieces over a moderate heat until browned and nearly cooked in the middle (almost 3 minutes each side). Remove the chicken pieces and set them aside. Put the onion, chillies (if used), garlic, ginger, nuts and soya sauce into a blender and blend them into a smooth paste, or use a pestle and mortar. Pour off from the wok or pan some of the oil the chicken was fried in, leaving only 2–3 tablespoons. Stir in the prepared paste, coriander, cumin and turmeric and stir fry the mixture for 2 minutes. Add the water or coconut milk, vinegar and sugar and stir the mixture well. Add salt to taste. Put in the chicken pieces and simmer uncovered until the chicken is tender and the sauce is thick (about 20–30 minutes).

Braised Chicken Balinese Style (Ayam Masak Bali)

Serves 6

This uses the same ingredients as fried chicken Balinese style above but the cooking method is different. The chicken is quickly and lightly fried in a spicy paste, water or coconut milk is then added and the chicken is simmered slowly until tender. Ingredients as for fried chicken Balinese style plus an extra 8 fl oz (225 ml) of water or coconut milk. Put the onion, chillies, garlic, ginger, almonds and soya sauce into the container of a blender and blend to a smooth paste, or use a pestle and mortar. Heat the oil in a wok or large pan and stir fry the prepared paste, coriander, cumin and turmeric for 2 minutes. Add the chicken pieces and lightly fry them on both sides. Add the water or coconut milk (making sure to use 16 fl oz/450 ml), vinegar and sugar and stir well. Add salt to taste. Bring the contents of the pan to the boil, reduce the heat, cover and simmer for 45 minutes or until the chicken is tender. Stir occasionally. If coconut milk is used rather than water do not cover the pan.

Spiced Boiled Chicken (Ayam Rebus Pedas)

Serves 6

A simple recipe in which the chicken is gently boiled with chillies, onion, lemon and tomato purée. It is easy to prepare and is suitable for rather tough pieces of chicken.

12 fl oz (350 ml) water

2–3 lb (1–1.5 kg) chicken cut into serving pieces *or* the same weight of chicken portions

2 medium onions, thinly sliced

2–4 fresh *or* dried red chillies, finely chopped

1 teaspoon grated lemon rind *or* 1 stalk lemon grass, chopped

1 tablespoon tomato purée

2 cloves garlic, crushed

salt to taste

1 tablespoon lemon juice

Put all the ingredients, except for the lemon juice, into a heavy saucepan. Bring to the boil, reduce the heat, cover and simmer the chicken gently for 50 minutes to 1 hour or until it is tender. Stir in the lemon juice, adjust the seasoning and serve with plain boiled rice and vegetables.

FISH DISHES
(Masakan Ikan)

In Indonesia there is an abundance of freshwater, marine fish and shell-fish which are important both in terms of the country's economy and in terms of the people's diet. Unlike elsewhere, there are no large fishing fleets but fishing is carried out on an individual or small community basis. The inland and inshore fishermen use small boats with an out-rigger, called prahus, or they stand waist-deep in the water and catch the fish in nets or traps. The deep sea fishermen take their large but basic sailing ships out to sea and stay there until they have made a large enough catch to make their journey worthwhile. The day's catch is sold on the day at the fish markets or otherwise it is sold off cheaply to be salted along with the fish, shrimps and prawns which are too small to sell fresh. Fish and shellfish are usually sold live, and prawns are by far the most popular shellfish in Indonesian cuisine. In fish restaurants you select your fish from live fish which are kept in tanks or small ponds.

There are many varieties of fish available in the markets and although some are familiar to Westerners – such as tuna, mullet and mackerel – most are not. You can use whatever fish is readily available for the recipes given here. Methods of cooking are various and include steaming, frying, grilling, poaching in coconut milk and currying.

Note that all grilled fish recipes are also suitable for barbecueing. Weights for whole fish given in the ingredients are cleaned fish weights. By cleaned, I mean the head cut off, the gut removed and the remaining fish rinsed well under cold water. I have normally not specified a particular fish in the recipes as most of the recipes lend themselves to most types of fish commonly available, both round and flat. For reference only, the following are the most commonly available fish in Indonesian markets:

Bawal (silver pomfret)
Cakalang (skipjack)
Karper (carp)
Ikan mas (golden freshwater carp)
Ikan pari (ray)
Bandeng (freshwater milk fish)
Kakap (giant perch)
Kakap merah (red snapper)
Tenggiri (Spanish mackerel)
Gurami (gurami)
Glodok (mud skipper)
Belut (eel).

Simple Grilled Fish (Ikan Panggang)

Serves 4

There are two methods for grilling fish. Method 1 is a simple grilling recipe suitable for any type of fish. Method 2 involves brushing the fish with a hot sour sauce and is best suited to strong-tasting fish which are cooked whole rather than in steaks.

2–3 lb (1–1.5 kg) total weight cleaned fish either 1 large whole fish *or* 4 small whole fish *or* 4 fish steaks *or* fillets vegetable oil	hot pepper sauce *or* sambal ulek dark soya sauce lemon juice salt

Method 1

Dry the fish, lightly brush it with oil and then cook it (or them) slowly over glowing charcoal or under a preheated grill, keeping the fish a fair distance from the heat source. Turn it (or them) occasionally and cook until the skin is nicely browned and the flesh is tender right to the centre. Season a small bowl of hot pepper sauce or sambal ulek with soya sauce and stir in some lemon juice. Serve the fish and gently dab each mouthful in the sauce before eating.

Method 2

Dry the fish and then rub it with salt and sprinkle with lemon juice. Make a paste from 1 tablespoon of hot pepper sauce or sambal ulek, 2 tablespoons of lemon juice, 2 tablespoons vegetable oil and 1 tablespoon soya sauce. Brush the fish with half of this paste and grill as in method 1. Halfway through the cooking time, brush the fish with the remaining paste. Serve when tender.

Marinated Grilled Fish with Sauce (Ikan Panggang Kecap)

Serves 4

This recipe is given for 1 large fish but it works equally well with smaller fish.

2–3 lb (1–1.5 kg) whole fish *or* 4
  small whole fish, cleaned
salt to taste
juice of ½ lemon

Marinade

2 cloves garlic, crushed
2 tablespoons dark soya sauce
2 teaspoons dark brown sugar
1 tablespoon water

Sauce
1 tablespoon melted butter
1 tablespoon dark soya sauce
juice of 1 lemon
1–2 fresh *or* dried red chillies,
  finely chopped
1 small onion, finely diced

Dry the fish, score the skin with a sharp knife and season it with salt. Sprinkle it with the juice of half the lemon. Prepare the marinade by combining the ingredients and mixing them well together. Put the fish in a dish and pour the marinade over it. Leave it to marinate for about 30 minutes to 1 hour. Remove the fish from the marinade, drain it, then grill it slowly over glowing charcoal or under a preheated grill, keeping it some distance from the heat source. During this time, baste the fish occasionally with any left-over marinade and turn it over now and again. Cook until the fish is browned and tender right to the centre. Serve the fish, pour over it the melted butter. Combine the remaining ingredients of the sauce and mix well, then pour the mixture over the fish.

Fried Fish with Sauce (Ikan Goreng)

Serves 4

This is a basic recipe but the fish is enhanced by serving the fried fish in one of a variety of sauces. Choose one from the five sauce recipes given below.

2–3 lb (1–1.5 kg) total weight
  cleaned fish either 1 large whole
  fish *or* 4 small whole fish *or* 4
  fish steaks *or* fillets
1 teaspoon cornflour

1 teaspoon salt
oil for deep or shallow frying

To garnish
lemon wedges

If using whole fish, score the skin 2 or 3 times on both sides with a sharp knife. Combine the cornflour and salt and sprinkle the mixture over the fish (and inside the cavity if using whole fish). Heat the oil and deep or shallow fry the fish until it is golden brown and tender. Serve with lemon wedges and/or one of the fried fish sauces below.

Sweet Spicy Sauce (Bumbu Manis)

2 tablespoons vegetable oil	2 teaspoons white sugar
2 medium onions, finely chopped	1 teaspoon grated lemon rind
2 cloves garlic, crushed	juice of 1 lemon
1–3 fresh *or* dried red chillies, finely chopped	2 tablespoons dark soya sauce
	8 fl oz (225 ml) water
1/2 teaspoon ground ginger *or* 1-in (2.5-cm) piece root ginger, grated	salt to taste

Heat the oil in a frying pan or wok and add the onions, garlic and chillies. Stir fry until the onions are softened. Add the ginger, sugar, lemon rind, lemon juice and soya sauce, stir the mixture well and cook it over a medium heat for 2–3 minutes. Add the water, mix it in well, bring the sauce to the boil, reduce the heat and simmer it for 15 minutes. Before serving, add salt to taste.

Sweet Spicy Tomato Sauce (Saos Tomat)

Ingredients as for sweet spicy sauce with the addition of 1 lb (450 g) ripe tomatoes, scalded in boiling water, peeled and chopped. Or use tinned tomatoes, chopped. Follow the recipe as above but add the tomatoes along with the ginger, sugar and other ingredients.

Black Bean Sauce (Saos Taoco)

Add 2 tablespoons black bean sauce to the sweet spicy sauce at the end of the cooking time, but before the salt has been added. Heat through and serve. Black bean sauce is salty and no extra salt is needed.

Tangy Onion Sauce (Bumbu Bawang)

2 tablespoons vegetable oil	3 medium onions, coarsely chopped
1 medium onion, finely diced	
2 cloves garlic, crushed	6 fl oz (175 ml) white vinegar
1/2 teaspoon ground turmeric	6 fl oz (175 ml) water
1–2 fresh *or* dried red chillies, chopped	salt and pepper to taste

Heat the oil in a heavy frying pan and stir fry the finely diced onion and garlic until lightly browned. Add the turmeric, chillies and stir fry for 1–2 minutes. Add the remaining ingredients, bring the mixture to the boil, stirring, reduce the heat and simmer until the onions are cooked. Taste for seasoning and adjust if necessary. If the sauce is a little too sour add 1–2 teaspoons white sugar.

Coconut and Peanut Sauce (Saos Kacang)

2 tablespoons crunchy peanut butter
4 fl oz (100 ml) fresh *or* canned coconut milk (for preparation from desiccated coconut see page 15)

2 tablespoons light soya sauce
1 tablespoon white vinegar

Combine all the ingredients and bring the mixture gently to the boil, stirring constantly. Pour over the fish and serve.

Lemon or Tamarind Fried Fish (Ikan Goreng)

Serves 4

There are two ways of doing this. In method 1 the fish is sprinkled with lemon juice and immediately fried. This is the easiest method to use with fish steaks or fillets. In method 2 the fish is marinated in a lemon juice marinade and this works best with whole fish. For a traditional Indonesian flavour replace the lemon juice with 3 tablespoons of tamarind water.

2–3 lb (1–1.5 kg) total weight cleaned fish either 1 large whole fish *or* 4 small whole fish *or* 4 fish steaks *or* fillets
salt and black pepper to taste
juice of 1 lemon
oil for frying

To garnish
tomato slices
lemon wedges
deep-fried onion slices (optional)

Method 1

If using a whole fish, score the skin 2 or 3 times on both sides. Season the fish or fish fillets with salt and black pepper and rub the seasonings in. Sprinkle the fish with fresh lemon juice. Heat the oil and deep fry the fish until golden brown and crispy or shallow fry it, turning once, until nicely browned. Serve the fish garnished.

Variation: Serve the fish with one of the fried fish sauces above.

Method 2

Mix the salt and black pepper with the lemon juice and add 10 fl oz (275 ml) of water. If using a whole fish score the skin 2 or 3 times on both sides. Marinate the fish or fish fillets in the lemon juice and water mixture and leave it for 30 minutes. Remove the fish and dry it. Heat the oil and deep fry the fish until golden brown and crispy or shallow fry, turning once, until nicely browned. Serve garnished.

Variation: Serve the fish with one of the fried fish sauces on pages 110–11.

Yellow Fried Fish (Ikan Bumbu Kuning)

Serves 4

2–3 lb (1–1.5 kg) total weight
   cleaned fish either 1 large whole
   fish *or* 4 small whole fish *or* 4
   fish steaks *or* fillets
1 teaspoon ground turmeric
2 teaspoons water

salt and black pepper to taste
oil for shallow frying

To garnish
lemon wedges

If using whole fish score the skin 2 or 3 times on both sides. In a bowl make a paste from the turmeric, water, salt and black pepper. Rub the fish evenly all over with this paste. Heat the oil in a heavy frying pan and gently fry the fish on both sides until tender. Serve with lemon wedges and, if you wish, with one of the fried fish sauces, recipes, on pages 110–11.

Vinegared Fried Fish (Ikan Cuka)

Serves 4

In this recipe the fish is shallow fried and then gently simmered in a vinegar sauce. The onions, garlic and ginger should remain a little crunchy.

2–3 lb (1–1.5 kg) total weight
   cleaned fish either 1 large whole
   fish *or* 4 small whole fish *or* 4
   fish steaks *or* fillets
1 teaspoon salt
1 teaspoon ground turmeric
oil for frying
3 small onions, quartered

2 cloves garlic, chopped
2-in (5-cm) piece root ginger,
   peeled and grated
1–2 fresh *or* dried red chillies,
   chopped
2 tablespoons white vinegar
12 fl oz (350 ml) water
salt to taste

Score the fish on both sides 2 or 3 times with a sharp knife. Combine the salt and turmeric and rub the mixture into the fish, inside and out. Shallow fry the fish until lightly browned on both sides. Set the fish aside. Add a little more oil to the frying pan and stir fry the onions, garlic, ginger and chillies for 1 minute. Add the vinegar and water and bring to the boil. Put in the fish. Simmer and add salt to taste. Remove the pan from the heat after 5 minutes and, ideally, leave the fish and sauce in the pan for 1 or 2 hours to allow the flavours to blend. Reheat and serve.

Fish in Soya Sauce (Ikan Kecap)

Serves 4

2 tablespoons vegetable oil
1 medium onion, finely chopped
2 cloves garlic, crushed
1–2 fresh *or* dried red chillies
1 teaspoon grated lemon rind *or* chopped lemon grass
2 lb (1 kg) fish fillets *or* steaks cut

into thick slices
2 tablespoons dark soya sauce
1 teaspoon white sugar
juice of 1 lemon
2 bay leaves *or* daun salem leaves
8 fl oz (225 ml) water
salt to taste

Heat the oil in a heavy frying pan or wok and add the onion, garlic, chillies and lemon rind or lemon grass. Stir fry until the onions are softened. Add the fish and fry it on both sides for 2–3 minutes. Add the soya sauce, sugar, lemon juice and bay leaves or daun salem leaves and fry a further 2 minutes. Pour in the water and add salt to taste, simmer, uncovered, until the fish is tender (about 10–12 minutes depending on the size of the slices).

Chilli Hot, Marinated, Baked or Grilled Fish (Ikan Bandeng Panggang)

Serves 4

Two marinades, one a ginger based one and the other soya sauce based have been given for this dish. Both marinades contain chilli peppers. Add more or less of them according to whether you want a hotter or milder dish.

2–3 lb (1–1.5 kg) total weight cleaned fish either 1 large whole fish *or* 4 small whole fish *or* 4 fish steaks *or* fillets

Marinade 1: Ginger and Chilli

2 fresh *or* dried red chillies,
  chopped
2-in (5-cm) piece ginger, peeled
  and chopped
4 cloves garlic

1 medium onion, chopped
juice of 1 lemon *or* lime
4 fl oz (100 ml) vegetable oil
salt to taste

Marinade 2: Soya Sauce and Chilli

2–3 fresh *or* dried red chillies,
  chopped
2 cloves garlic

6 fl oz (175 ml) dark soya sauce
juice of 1 lemon *or* lime
2 tablespoons vegetable oil

If using whole fish make diagonal incisions on each side of the thickest part of the fish. Arrange the fish in a casserole dish. Put the chosen marinade ingredients in a blender and blend the mixture to a smooth paste. Brush or rub the fish on both sides with all of the paste and leave it to marinate for 1 hour. Preheat oven to 350 F (180 C, gas mark 4). Cover the casserole dish and bake the fish for 15–20 minutes for small fish or fish fillets and up to 30 minutes for large fish. Serve hot with rice and pickles. Alternatively grill the marinated fish over charcoal or under a grill on both sides until tender. During cooking, baste it with marinade from the dish and serve any that is left over in a separate bowl.

Variation: Another way of cooking this meal is to wrap the fish, with marinade spooned over it, in lightly greased pieces of foil (traditionally banana leaves are used) place the wrapped fish in a dish and bake it in a preheated oven at 350° F (180° C, gas mark 4) for 15–20 minutes, for small fish and up to 30 minutes for a large fish.

Spiced Stuffed Baked Fish (Ikan Isi)

Serves 4

2–3 lb (1–1.5 kg) total weight
  cleaned fish
4 oz (100 g) fish fillets (for the
  stuffing)
1 medium onion, finely chopped
2 cloves garlic
2 teaspoons ground coriander
1 teaspoon ground cumin

1/2 teaspoon cayenne powder
1/2 teaspoon ground turmeric
salt to taste
2 tablespoons dark soya sauce
juice of 1 lemon
3 tablespoons vegetable oil
1 fresh *or* dried chilli pepper, finely
  chopped (optional)

Preheat the oven to 350 F (180 C, gas mark 4). Put the fish fillet, onion, garlic, coriander, cumin, cayenne, turmeric and salt in a blender and blend to a smooth paste, or finely chop the fillet, onion and garlic and crush them and the spices to a paste in a pestle and mortar. Pack the cavity of the fish with the paste filling and then sew it closed or fasten with a couple of skewers. Place it in a casserole dish. Combine the soya sauce, lemon juice, oil and chilli pepper and pour this mixture over the fish. Put the dish, uncovered, in the preheated oven and bake for 20–30 minutes, depending on the size of the fish.

Fried Fish Baked in Coconut Milk (Ikan Panggang Santan)

Serves 4

In this recipe the fish is deep fried in oil and then baked in spicy coconut milk. The size of the deep frying pan will dictate the size of the fish that can be cooked. In Indonesia they would use 1 large fish but 2–4 smaller whole fish are just as satisfactory. White fish such as cod, haddock or plaice are best for this recipe.

2–3 lb (1–1.5 kg) fish, cleaned and dried 1 large *or* 4 small
oil for deep frying
4 fl oz (100 ml) water
1–2 fresh *or* dried red chillies, chopped
1/2 teaspoon ground turmeric
1 teaspoon ground cumin
1/2 teaspoon ground coriander
1/2 teaspoon ground ginger
8 fl oz (225 ml) fresh *or* canned coconut milk
2 medium onions, finely sliced
salt to taste
juice of 1 lemon

Preheat the oven to 350 F (180 C, gas mark 4). Heat the oil and deep fry the fish in it until nicely browned. Remove the fish, drain them and place them in a baking dish. Put the water, chillies, turmeric, cumin, coriander and ginger into a blender and blend them to a smooth paste. If the paste is too thin add a little desiccated coconut (lightly dry fried) to thicken it up. Brush the fish with this paste on both sides, put the sliced onion on top of the fish. Pour in the coconut milk, add salt and lemon juice. Cover the fish and bake in a preheated oven for 20–30 minutes, or until the fish is tender.

Wrapped Fish Grilled or Baked
(Ikan Pepes Bakar)

Serves 4

In this recipe the fish are marinated, then wrapped in banana leaves or, in the Western kitchen, aluminium foil. They are then grilled or baked until tender. This method produces moist, succulent fish.

Recipes are given for different marinades. Choose whichever you prefer. Marinade 1 is sweet and sour while marinade 2 is chilli and garlic based.

2–3 lb (1–1.5 kg) total weight cleaned fish, either 1 large whole fish *or* 4 small whole fish *or* 4 fish steaks *or* fillets

salt to taste
2 lemons, sliced

Marinade 1: Sweet and Sour

1 tablespoon vegetable oil
2 cloves garlic
1 medium onion, sliced
2-in (5-cm) piece root ginger, peeled and chopped
2 tablespoons tamarind water *or* lemon juice

1 fresh *or* dried chilli, seeded and chopped
1 tablespoon dark soya sauce
1 teaspoon brown sugar
1/2 teaspoon ground turmeric
salt to taste

Marinade 2: Chilli and Garlic

4 cloves garlic
3–4 fresh *or* dried red chillies, seeded, chopped
1/2 teaspoon ground turmeric

juice of 1 lemon
1 teaspoon grated lemon peel *or* 1 stalk lemon grass
2 tablespoons dark soya sauce

Lightly score the flesh of the fish, season with salt and place in a shallow dish. Combine the ingredients for whichever marinade you're going to use in a blender and blend the mixture to a smooth paste. Pour this paste over the fish and leave to marinate for 30 minutes. If you are going to bake the fish preheat the oven to 425° F (220° C, gas mark 7). Take the fish from the marinade and place each on a piece of foil big enough to wrap it in (or use large banana leaves). Smear the fish with some marinade and then place 2–3 lemon slices on top of each. Wrap each fish and keep the seam side underneath. Reserve marinade that's left and serve it as a side sauce. Bake the wrapped fish in the preheated oven for 20 minutes, turning the packets over halfway through the cooking time. Place the wrapped fish on a serving dish, seams uppermost and open them at the table. Serve with rice, vegetables and sambals.

Alternatively, you can grill the wrapped fish over glowing charcoal or under a preheated domestic grill on a medium setting for 10 minutes each side. Serve.

Steamed Fish (Ikan Pepes Kukas)

Serves 4

Prepare the marinated fish as described in the above recipe, to the point where they are ready to be wrapped and cooked. Place them unwrapped in a steamer and steam for 20 minutes. Serve with rice, vegetables and sambals. If you do not have a fish steamer a good substitute is a plate on top of an upturned basin or bowl. Put the fish on the plate and put the basin with the plate on top in a large saucepan containing about 2 in (5 cm) water. Boil the water, reduce it to a steady simmer and steam the fish until cooked. Make sure that there is enough water in the saucepan.

Fish Curry (Ikan Kari)

Serves 4

Fish curry can be made with most types of fish although firm-fleshed fish that can be cut into small slices or cubes are the best.

1½ lb (750 g) fish fillets *or* fish steaks cut into 2-in (5-cm) cubes
juice of 1 lemon
2 tablespoons vegetable oil
2 medium onions, sliced
2 cloves garlic, crushed
2 teaspoons ground coriander
1 teaspoon ground turmeric

2-in (5-cm) piece root ginger, finely sliced *or* ½ teaspoon ground ginger
½ teaspoon chilli powder
12 fl oz (350 ml) fresh *or* canned coconut milk
8 oz (225 g) tomatoes, peeled, quartered
salt and pepper to taste

Sprinkle lemon juice from half the lemon over the fish and set it aside. Heat the oil in a frying pan or wok and stir fry the onions and garlic until lightly browned. Add the coriander, turmeric, ginger and chilli powder and stir fry for a further 1–2 minutes. Add the fish pieces and remaining lemon juice and mix well. Pour in the coconut milk, add the tomatoes and salt and pepper to taste. Stir well and gently simmer, stirring occasionally, until the fish is cooked (about 15 minutes). Serve with boiled rice and sliced cucumber.

Fish Poached in Coconut Milk (Ikan Santan)

Serves 4

2 lb (1 kg) fish fillets *or* steaks, cut into large pieces
salt
1 lemon
1¼ pints (700 ml) fresh *or* canned coconut milk
3 cloves garlic, crushed
2-in (5-cm) piece root ginger, peeled, finely sliced *or* ½ teaspoon ground ginger

2 teaspoons crunchy peanut butter
1 medium onion, finely sliced
1 fresh *or* dried red chilli, finely chopped *or* ½ teaspoon chilli powder
½ teaspoon turmeric
salt to taste

Season the fish pieces with salt and sprinkle them with the juice of half the lemon. Set them aside. Put all the remaining ingredients in a large saucepan and gently bring the mixture to the boil, stirring constantly. Reduce the heat and simmer gently for 30 minutes. Add the fish and the juice and grated lemon rind of the unused half lemon. Gently bring to the boil, stirring, then reduce the heat to a simmer and cook, stirring occasionally until the fish is tender (10–15 minutes).

Fish Poached in Tamarind or Lemon Juice (Ikan Pindang)

Serves 4

4 herrings *or* mackerel (total weight 2–3 lb/1–1.5 kg), heads left on
2 tablespoons vegetable oil
4 cloves garlic, crushed
1 medium onion, finely chopped
1 fresh *or* dried red chilli, chopped *or* ½ teaspoon chilli powder

1 tablespoon dark brown sugar
4 fl oz (100 ml) tamarind water *or* lemon juice
16 fl oz (450 ml) water
salt to taste

To garnish
lemon wedges

Thoroughly rinse the fish under cold water and, if you wish to, cut off the heads (Indonesians leave the heads on and find it very strange that

Westerners do not appreciate this part of the fish). Set the fish in a large saucepan. Heat the oil in a frying pan and lightly fry the garlic, onion and chilli pepper or powder, sugar, tamarind water or lemon juice, and water. Add salt to taste and bring to the boil. Pour this mixture over the fish in the pan and bring to the boil. Cover the pan, reduce the heat to a low simmer and cook for about 20 minutes or until the fish is tender, and the sauce has thickened. If, towards the end of the cooking period, the sauce has not thickened enough remove the lid and simmer the fish uncovered. Serve the fish with the sauce and garnish with lemon wedges.

Spiced Poached Fish (Ikan Pangek)

Serves 4

1 tablespoon oil
2 medium onions, finely chopped
2 cloves garlic, crushed
2–3 fresh *or* dried red chillies, finely chopped
1 teaspoon ground turmeric
1 pint (550 ml) water
2 lb (1 kg) fish fillets cut into 8 pieces

1 teaspoon brown sugar
juice of 2 lemons
2 bay leaves *or* daun salem leaves
2 teaspoons grated lemon rind *or* chopped lemon grass
salt to taste

To garnish
cucumber slices

Lightly smear a large saucepan or frying pan with oil and add the onions, garlic, chillies and turmeric and stir fry over a moderate heat for 2–3 minutes. Add the water and bring the mixture to the boil. Leave it to boil gently for 5 minutes. Put in the fish, sugar, lemon juice, bay leaves or daun salem leaves, lemon rind or lemon grass and salt. Cover and cook, simmering, for 20–30 minutes, depending on the size of the fish pieces, or until the sauce has thickened and the fish is tender. Serve garnished with cucumber slices.

Fish in Sweet and Sour Sauce (Ikan Asam Manis)

Serves 4

2 lb (1 kg) fish fillets *or* 4 small whole fish, cleaned, skin scored 2–3 times with a sharp knife

salt
juice of 1 lemon
oil for shallow frying

Sauce

2 tablespoons oil
1 medium onion, finely sliced
2 cloves garlic, crushed
1–2 fresh *or* dried red chillies,
     seeded and finely chopped

8 oz (225 g) ripe tomatoes, peeled
     and chopped
1/2 teaspoon ground turmeric
1/4 teaspoon ground ginger
2 teaspoons white sugar
2 tablespoons white vinegar
8 fl oz (225 ml) water
salt

Season the fish with salt, sprinkle it with lemon juice and set it aside.
To make the sauce: heat 2 tablespoons of oil in a saucepan and sauté the
onion, garlic and chillies for 2–3 minutes. Add the tomatoes,
turmeric, ginger, sugar and vinegar and stir and cook for 1–2 minutes.
Add the water and salt and simmer it for 15 minutes. Meanwhile, heat
the oil and shallow fry the fish on both sides until well-browned and
tender. Put the fish on a serving dish, cover with the sauce and serve.

Indonesian Fish Salad
(Ikan Sardin Tumis Tomat)

Serves 4 as a starter or side dish

This colourful and tasty salad is a good way of brightening up a tin of
sardines or other tinned fish.

12 oz (350 g) sardines *or* pilchards
     tinned in tomato sauce *or* oil
4 oz (100 g) tomatoes, sliced
1/2 small cucumber, peeled,
     deseeded, diced

8 oz (225 g) tinned *or* fresh
     pineapple, cubed
1 small onion, diced
1–2 fresh *or* dried red chillies,
     chopped
salt and black pepper to taste

In a bowl combine the ingredients, mix them together well and serve.

PRAWN DISHES
(Masakan Udang)

Before cooking large prawns, rinse, shell and devein them, leaving the tail intact. The vein along the back of the prawn must always be removed since the stomach and its contents, if eaten, may be poisonous. The tail is left on to provide a convenient way of picking up the cooked prawn.

To shell and devein a prawn cut open the shell along the back with a sharp, pointed knife, leaving the tail section uncut. Remove the shell and legs. With the knife point pick out the vein along the back. For those recipes in which the tail has to be removed, hold the prawn by the body and with the finger and thumb gently squeeze and pull the tail at the same time. It should come off easily.

Frozen or tinned prawns can be substituted for fresh ones in the recipes given here but if fresh prawns are available they are the best.

Fried Prawns (Udang Goreng)

Serves 4 as a starter or side dish

The first method of preparing prawns involves coating them in batter and deep frying; in the second, they are dipped in egg and bread-crumbs before being deep fried.

Method 1

1 lb (450 g) large prawns, shelled   4 oz (100 g) plain flour
   and deveined   1 egg, beaten
juice of ½ lemon   6 fl oz (175 ml) milk
salt and pepper to taste   oil for deep frying

Sprinkle the prawns with lemon juice and season them to taste with
salt and pepper. Beat together the flour, egg, milk and salt to form a
smooth batter. Heat the oil. Dip the prawns into the batter and deep
fry them 3 or 4 at a time. Drain on absorbent paper and serve.

Method 2

1 lb (450 g) large prawns, shelled   salt and pepper to taste
   and deveined   breadcrumbs *or* plain flour *or*
2 eggs, beaten   cornflour for coating
½ teaspoon ground coriander   oil for deep frying
¼ teaspoon ground cumin

Add the coriander, cumin, salt and pepper to the eggs and mix well.
Dip the prawns into this mixture and then coat them with bread-
crumbs or flour. Heat the oil. Deep fry the prawns in it 3 or 4 at a time.
Drain on absorbent paper and serve.

Marinated Sour Fried Prawns
(Udang Goreng Asam)

Serves 4 as a starter or side dish

1 lb (450 g) large prawns, shelled   2 cloves garlic, crushed
   and deveined   salt to taste
4 tablespoons tamarind water *or*   1 egg, beaten
   lemon juice   breadcrumbs *or* plain flour for
½ teaspoon ground ginger   coating
¼ teaspoon ground turmeric   oil for deep frying

In a bowl, combine the tamarind water or lemon juice with the ginger,
turmeric, garlic and salt. Add the prawns and leave them to marinate
for 30 minutes. Remove the prawns from the marinade, dip them in
the beaten egg and coat them with breadcrumbs or flour. Heat the oil
and deep fry the prawns 3 or 4 at a time until nicely browned. Drain on
absorbent paper and serve.

Deep Fried Prawns in Tomato Sauce (Udang Saos Tomat)

Serves 4 as a starter or side dish

1 lb (450 g) large prawns, shelled
  and deveined
salt and pepper to taste
2 eggs, beaten
breadcrumbs *or* plain flour *or*
  cornflour for coating
oil for deep frying

Sauce
2 tablespoons vegetable oil
2 cloves garlic, crushed

1 small onion, diced
2-in (5-cm) piece root ginger,
  peeled and grated
1 fresh *or* dried red chilli, chopped
8 oz (225 g) ripe tomatoes, peeled
  and chopped *or* tinned tomatoes,
  sliced
1 tablespoon dark soya sauce
2 teaspoons white sugar
4 fl oz (100 ml) water
salt to taste

Sprinkle the prawns with salt and pepper. Set them aside and prepare the sauce. Heat the oil in a frying pan or wok and stir fry the garlic, onion, root ginger and chilli until the onion is softened. Add the tomatoes, soya sauce, sugar, water and salt, stir well and simmer until the tomatoes have disintegrated. Dip the prawns in the beaten egg and roll them in breadcrumbs or flour. Heat the oil and deep fry the prawns 3 or 4 at a time until golden brown. Serve the deep fried prawns covered with tomato sauce.

Curried Prawns (Udang Masak Bumbu)

Serves 4 as a starter or side dish

2 tablespoons vegetable oil
2 medium onions, sliced
2 cloves garlic, crushed
1–2 fresh *or* dried red chillies,
  chopped
1 teaspoon ground coriander
1/2 teaspoon ground cumin

1/2 teaspoon ground turmeric
1/2 teaspoon ground ginger
1 pint (550 ml) water
1 lb (450 g) large prawns, shelled
  and deveined
2 teaspoons white sugar
salt to taste

Heat the oil in a wok or frying pan and stir fry the onions, garlic and chillies in it until just softened. Add the coriander, cumin, turmeric and ginger and stir fry for a further minute. Add the water, mix well and bring to the boil. Put in the prawns and remaining ingredients and simmer, uncovered, for 20 minutes or so until the prawns are tender and the sauce has thickened.

Fried Prawns in Spiced Coconut Milk (Sambal Goreng Udang)

Serves 4 as a starter or side dish

1 small onion, diced
2 cloves garlic
2 red chillies, fresh *or* dried *or* 1
  teaspoon chilli powder
1-in (2.5-cm) piece root ginger,
  peeled, chopped
1 teaspoon ground coriander

1 tablespoon vegetable oil
1 lb (450 g) prawns, shelled and
  deveined
4 fl oz (100 ml) fresh *or* canned
  coconut milk
salt to taste

Put the onion, garlic, chillies, ginger, coriander and oil into a blender and blend the mixture to a smooth paste. Heat a frying pan or wok and add the paste. Gently fry and stir the mixture until it has browned. Add the prawns and coat them with the paste. Add the coconut milk and salt. Stir and boil very gently until the prawns are tender and the sauce is thick and dark.

Spiced Fried Prawns (Udang Goreng Bumbu)

Serves 4 as a starter or side dish

Prepare the same spice paste as in the previous recipe (do not fry it). Rub 1 lb (450 g) prawns, shelled and deveined, with the paste and set them aside to marinate for 2–4 hours. Heat the oil and shallow fry the prawns in it until lightly browned. Serve. They are very hot, so be careful!

VEGETABLE DISHES
(Masakan Sayur)

In Indonesian cooking, vegetables are always prepared with care and whatever cooking technique is used, the basic aim is to retain the texture and colour of the individual vegetables. Parboiling, light steaming and stir frying are the most popular cooking methods used. The dishes given here can be roughly divided into four types. Firstly there are those in which the vegetables, either lightly cooked or raw, are served with a sauce poured over them; secondly, stir-fried dishes; thirdly, curried dishes and finally, thin vegetable stews.

Most of the recipes in the first part of the chapter can be applied to whatever vegetable or combination of vegetables you like; the vegetables in the ingredients columns are simply suggestions. However, the recipes in the last part of the chapter are for specific vegetables.

Mixed Vegetable Salad with Peanut Sauce (Gado-gado)

Serves 4

Gado-gado is one of my favourite Indonesian dishes. It is crunchy, tasty and good for you. It makes a good light lunch or with rice and other side dishes, an excellent vegetarian meal. A mixture of raw and cooked vegetables are arranged on a serving dish and a spicy peanut sauce is either served with them or poured over the top before serving. The recipe I have given is a general one and you may substitute your own selection of vegetables. The cooked vegetables (except the potatoes) are only parboiled and should retain their texture and colour. Gado-gado can be served hot or cold.

Vegetables

1/2 medium cucumber, thickly sliced

4 oz (100 g) beansprouts, washed, drained

1/2 lettuce, washed and chopped *or* 1 small bunch watercress

2 medium carrots, sliced lengthwise, parboiled

2 medium potatoes, peeled and boiled until just cooked, sliced

3 oz (75 g) cabbage leaves, lightly blanched in boiling water, chopped

4 oz (100 g) green or French beans, stringed, cut into 2-in (5-cm) lengths, parboiled

Sauce

2 tablespoons vegetable oil

2 cloves garlic, crushed

1–3 (according to taste) fresh *or* dried red chillies, finely sliced, *or* 1/2–1 1/2 teaspoons chilli powder

1 medium onion, finely diced

8 oz (225 g) roasted peanuts, crushed *or* milled in a food blender *or* 8 oz (225 g) crunchy peanut butter

1 tablespoon brown sugar

1 tablespoon lemon juice

16 fl oz (450 ml) water

salt to taste

To garnish

choose from:

1 hard-boiled egg, sliced

2 medium onions, thinly sliced and fried crisp and brown in a little oil

prawn crackers

To make the sauce, heat the oil in a saucepan or wok and add the garlic, chillies or chilli powder and onion and stir fry the mixture over a moderate heat until the onion is golden. Add the crushed peanuts or peanut butter, sugar, lemon juice and water, stir well and bring it all to a gentle boil. Reduce the heat and simmer, stirring occasionally, until the sauce has thickened but remains thin enough to pour. Add salt to taste. Keep the sauce hot on a very low simmer. Prepare and arrange the vegetables on a serving dish, pour the sauce over (or serve it in a separate bowl) and garnish the top with slices of hard-boiled egg and fried onions. Serve with prawn crackers if available.

Variations

1. Bean curd, cubed and shallow or deep fried, is often included in the vegetable salad part of the dish.
2. Prawn paste (1 teaspoon) or anchovy sauce (1 teaspoon) added to the peanut sauce (at the same time as the lemon juice) gives it a traditional Indonesian flavour.

Vegetable Curry (Kari Sayur)

Serves 4

This recipe can be used for a single vegetable or a combination of vegetables. I have given some suggestions as to what you might use. If you choose more than one vegetable, always add to the pot the ones that take the longest to cook first. For example, potatoes would obviously be added before broccoli.

1 lb (450 g) total weight vegetables. Select one or more from:
potatoes, peeled, diced
aubergines, cubed, rinsed, drained
young peas in the pod, leave whole
green or French beans, stringed, chopped
celery, chopped
cabbage, coarsely shredded
cauliflower, cut into florets
green or red pepper, cored, seeded, cut into strips
broccoli, chopped
kale, chopped
beansprouts, washed
plus
2 tablespoons vegetable oil

1 medium onion, finely diced
2–3 cloves garlic, crushed
2–3 fresh or dried red or green chillies, finely chopped or 1 teaspoon chilli powder
1 teaspoon ground coriander
1/2 teaspoon ground cumin
1/2 teaspoon ground ginger
1/2 teaspoon ground turmeric
5 almonds or macadamia nuts, chopped
salt and pepper to taste
16 fl oz (450 ml) fresh or canned coconut milk (to prepare from desiccated coconut see page 15) or 12 fl oz (350 ml) water and 4 oz (100 g) desiccated coconut
juice of 1 lemon

Heat the oil in a large frying pan or wok and stir fry the onion, garlic, chillies or chilli powder, coriander, cumin, ginger, turmeric, chopped nuts, salt and pepper over a moderate heat. Continue cooking until the onions are softened. Add the coconut milk or water and desiccated coconut and stir the mixture well, bringing it to a gentle boil. Now start adding the vegetables, adding those that take longest to cook first. Simmer, stirring regularly until all the vegetables are cooked but not soggy. Stir in the lemon juice, adjust the seasoning if necessary and serve.

Mixed Vegetable Salad with Coconut Sauce (Urap)

Serves 4

Urap is similar to gado-gado but has a coconut sauce. It can be made with any combination of vegetables and they can be cooked or uncooked. If the vegetables are cooked they should either be lightly steamed or parboiled so that the full colour and texture of the vegetables is retained. I have given recipes for two uncooked coconut sauces and one for a cooked sauce. The first uncooked sauce uses fresh, grated coconut and the second desiccated coconut. The second, as far as ingredients are concerned, is probably easier to prepare in a Western kitchen. There is also a recipe for a cooked coconut sauce which can be served hot with cooked vegetables.

1 lb (450 g) total weight of one or more types of lightly cooked or raw vegetables, chopped, shredded or sliced. The following are suggestions:
aubergines, cubed, rinsed, drained, steamed until tender
green or French beans, stringed, chopped, parboiled

carrots, sliced, parboiled *or* raw, grated
green *or* red peppers, seeded and cut into strips, served raw *or* parboiled
cucumber, peeled, seeded, diced
courgettes, sliced

(See gado-gado and vegetable curry recipes on pages 126–27 for other vegetable suggestions and methods of cutting.)

Urap with Uncooked Sauce

Serves 4

either	or
4 oz (100 g) fresh coconut, grated	4 oz (100 g) desiccated coconut
1 clove garlic, crushed	2 tablespoons hot water
1 teaspoon brown sugar	1/2 onion, finely diced
1–2 fresh *or* dried red chillies, finely sliced	1/2 teaspoon chilli powder
	2 cloves garlic, crushed
1/2 teaspoon prawn paste	juice of 1 lemon
salt to taste	1/2 teaspoon prawn paste (optional)

Prepare either sauce by combining the ingredients and mixing them well together. Combine the sauce with the prepared vegetables, toss the salad and serve immediately.

Urap with Cooked Sauce

Serves 4

2 cloves garlic	6 oz (175 g) desiccated coconut
1 medium onion, chopped	4 fl oz (100 ml) water
1–2 fresh *or* dried red chillies	1 teaspoon brown sugar
1/2 teaspoon prawn paste (optional)	salt to taste

Put the garlic, onion, chillies and prawn paste (if used) into a blender and blend the mixture to a smooth paste. Put the coconut in a bowl and stir in the water, sugar and add salt to taste. Mix in the spice paste. Stand the bowl on another upturned bowl in a pan containing about 1 in (2.5 cm) of water. Boil the water and steam the coconut sauce for 20 minutes. Meanwhile, prepare your vegetables and combine them into a salad. Toss the salad in the hot or cold sauce and serve. Hot sauce is normally best with cooked vegetables and cold sauce with raw vegetables.

Green Salad with Coconut Sauce (Slada Saos Kelapa)

Prepare a green salad from a selection of vegetables in season, for example, lettuce, cabbage, Chinese cabbage, watercress, spinach (lightly cooked), French or green beans (sliced and parboiled), young peas in their pods. Make one of the coconut sauces from the urap recipe above and toss the salad in it. Serve.

Stir Fried Vegetables (Sayur Tumis)

Serves 4

This recipe can be used for one or a combination of vegetables. If using more than one vegetable, add those vegetables that take the longest to cook to the pan first.

1 lb (450 g) total weight washed and chopped vegetables. Select one or more from:

French or green beans, stringed, chopped

carrots, sliced

celery, chopped

beansprouts

cabbage, shredded

green *or* red peppers, seeded, cored and sliced

courgettes, sliced

(See vegetable curry recipe on page 127 for other suggestions.)

plus

2 tablespoons vegetable oil

1 clove garlic, crushed

1 small onion, finely sliced

2 bay leaves *or* daun salem leaves

1 teaspoon grated lemon peel *or* 1 stalk lemon grass, chopped

¼ teaspoon prawn paste *or* anchovy essence (optional)

2 teaspoons dark soya sauce

salt to taste

Heat the oil in a wok or pan and add the garlic, onion, bay leaves or daun salem leaves, lemon peel and prawn paste (if used). Stir fry the mixture until the onion is softened. Add the vegetable or mixed vegetables (in the correct cooking order, the hardest first) and stir fry until they are lightly cooked but still crunchy. Add soya sauce and then, if necessary, salt to taste. Stir well and serve.

Variations: For chilli hot vegetables add 1 or 2 fresh or dried chillies, finely chopped with the garlic, onion and other spices. Raw peanuts, 4 oz (100 g), are also good when fried along with the vegetables.

Sour Vegetables (Sayur Asam)

Serves 4

This dish is similar in consistency to a soup but it is thought of by the Indonesians as a dish of parboiled vegetables in a thin sauce. It is served with rice which complements the dish perfectly. The sour taste of sayur asam comes from the addition of tamarind water. Lemon juice can be substituted.

1 small onion, finely diced
2 cloves garlic, crushed
1 small red *or* green chilli, finely
chopped *or* 1/2 teaspoon chilli
powder
5 almonds *or* macadamia nuts,
crushed
16 fl oz (450 ml) water *or* stock
8 oz (225 g) raw peanuts
2 bay leaves *or* daun salem leaves

4 oz (100 g) green or French beans
cut into 1-in (2.5-cm) lengths
1 medium aubergine, cubed,
salted, washed and drained
2 medium courgettes, sliced
4 cabbage leaves, coarsely chopped
4 tablespoons tamarind water *or*
lemon juice
salt to taste

Put the onion, garlic, chilli, nuts and half the water or stock into a blender and blend the mixture to a thin paste. Transfer the paste to a small pan and bring it to the boil and simmer for 5 minutes. Meanwhile, put the peanuts, bay leaves or daun salem leaves and remaining water in another pan and boil this mixture for 5 minutes. Combine the contents of the two pans and put in the green or French beans. Simmer for 3–4 minutes and then add the aubergines and courgettes. Simmer for 5 minutes and add the cabbage leaves, tamarind water or lemon juice and salt. Simmer for a further 5 minutes or until all the vegetables are just tender and then serve.

Vegetables and Coconut Baked with Egg (Urap Panggang)

In this variation of the urap recipe (see page 128), the vegetables are fried with spices and desiccated coconut and then mixed with beaten egg and baked. I have suggested a combination of courgettes and aubergines but other vegetables may be substituted.

8 oz (225 g) aubergines, cubed
8 oz (225 g) courgettes, thinly
sliced
salt
2 tablespoons vegetable oil
1 small onion, thinly sliced
2 cloves garlic, crushed
1 fresh *or* dried red chilli, seeded,
finely chopped

1 teaspoon coriander seeds,
crushed
1-in (2.5-cm) piece root ginger,
finely chopped
6 oz (175 g) desiccated coconut *or*
freshly grated coconut
8 fl oz (225 ml) water
2 medium eggs, beaten
pepper to taste

Sprinkle the aubergines and courgettes with salt and leave to stand for 20 minutes. Rinse them under running water and pat them dry on kitchen paper. Heat the oil in a frying pan or wok, add the onion and garlic and stir fry for 1 minute. Add the courgettes, aubergines, chilli, coriander and root ginger and stir fry for 2–3 minutes. Stir in the coconut and continue frying for another 2 minutes. Add the water, stir well, reduce the heat and simmer for 5 minutes. Meanwhile, preheat the oven to 350°F (180°C, gas mark 4). Put the contents of the pan into an ovenproof dish and pour in the beaten eggs. Stir gently to distribute the egg evenly. Add salt and pepper to taste and put the dish in the oven. Bake uncovered for 30 minutes or until the egg is set. Serve.

Vinegared Mixed Vegetables (Acar Kuning)

Serves 8 as a side dish

Vegetables are parboiled in a spicy vinegar dressing, coloured yellow with turmeric to give a fresh crunchy salad pickle. It can be eaten straightaway or will keep for up to a week in a refrigerator. Serve as a side dish with main meals and salads. Other vegetables than those suggested can be used, for example, sliced celery, chopped tomatoes (the greenish variety) or beansprouts. Variations of this dish are popular all over Indonesia.

2 tablespoons vegetable oil
2 cloves garlic, crushed
1 small onion, finely sliced
1/2 teaspoon ground turmeric
1–2 fresh *or* dried red chillies, left whole
1-in (2.5-cm) piece root ginger, peeled and sliced *or* 1/2 teaspoon ground ginger
1 teaspoon cumin seeds, crushed
1 medium green *or* red pepper, seeded, decored, cut into strips
either
3 oz (75 g) French beans, cut into 1-in (2.5-cm) lengths

3 oz (75 g) carrots, peeled, cut into matchsticks
4 oz (100 g) cabbage, coarsely chopped
4 oz (100 g) courgettes, finely sliced
or
1 lb (450 g) of only one of the above vegetables
4 tablespoons white vinegar
1 teaspoon sugar
6 fl oz (175 ml) water
salt to taste

Heat the oil in a saucepan and fry the garlic and onion until golden. Stir in the turmeric, chillies, ginger and cumin and cook, stirring, for 1 minute. Add the vegetables, vinegar, sugar, water and salt. Cook, stirring, until the vegetables are just tender but still crunchy. Serve immediately.

Variation: The vegetables, if not absolutely fresh, can be stir fried for 2–3 minutes in the onion and garlic spice mixture before the vinegar, sugar and water are added.

Cooked Vegetable Salad with Peanut Dressing (Pecel)

Serves 4

This is a simple but effective recipe in which fresh young vegetables are lightly cooked then cooled and covered in a peanut-based dressing. The combination of vegetables given in the recipe is only a suggestion and it could be replaced with other combinations of your own taste. Two recipes for peanut sauce are given. The first is hot and spicy and the second is mild.

4 oz (100 g) carrots, coarsely chopped
4 oz (100 g) French beans cut into 2-in (5-cm) lengths
4 oz (100 g) cabbage, shredded

4 oz (100 g) beansprouts
2 medium potatoes, boiled until just tender and sliced
1 cucumber, peeled, cut in half lengthwise, deseeded, sliced

Sauce 1

4 oz (100 g) peanuts, roasted and crushed *or* 4 oz (100 g) crunchy peanut butter
1–2 fresh *or* dried red chillies, finely chopped
1 tablespoon lemon juice
1 teaspoon brown sugar

salt to taste
4 tablespoons hot water
1 tablespoon vegetable oil

To garnish
1 medium onion, finely sliced

Cook the carrots, beans, cabbage, beansprouts and cucumber separately in gently boiling water for 3–5 minutes each. They should remain crunchy in texture. Drain and mix the vegetables with the cooked potato slices and place the mixture onto a serving dish. To make the sauce, mix the crushed peanuts, chillies, lemon juice, sugar and salt with enough hot water to form a thick sauce that just runs off a spoon. Beat the sauce with a fork or in a blender. Fry the onion slices in the oil until browned and crisp. Pour the peanut sauce over the mixed vegetables and garnish the dish with fried onions.

Sauce 2

4 oz (100 g) peanuts, roasted and crushed *or* 4 oz (100 g) peanut butter
1 clove garlic

½ small onion, diced
1 teaspoon brown sugar
4 tablespoons hot water
salt to taste

Put all the ingredients into the container of a blender and blend them to a smooth paste. Serve on the vegetables as sauce 1 above.

Mixed Vegetables in Coconut Milk (Sayur Lodeh)

Serves 4

Sayur lodeh is thin and soupy. It is served with boiled rice and other main dishes. The rice is moistened with liquid from the sayur before being eaten. As with the other recipes in this section, any seasonal vegetable can be used. I have given a suggested combination which illustrates the order in which vegetables with different cooking times should be added to the pan.

2 tablespoons vegetable oil
1 small onion, finely diced
2 cloves garlic, crushed
1 red chilli, finely chopped *or* ½
    teaspoon chilli powder
1 teaspoon prawn paste (optional)
    or 1 teaspoon anchovy essence
    (optional)
16 fl oz (450 ml) fresh *or* canned
    coconut milk

4 oz (100 g) French beans cut into
    1-in (2.5-cm) lengths
4 oz (100 g) aubergines, cubed,
    salted, rinsed, drained
1 teaspoon grated lemon rind
10 fl oz (350 ml) stock *or* water
4 oz (100 g) cabbage, coarsely
    shredded
salt

Heat the oil in a heavy saucepan, add the onion and garlic and sauté until the onion is softened. Add the chilli, prawn paste (if used) and lemon rind and stir and cook the mixture for 2–3 minutes. Make sure the prawn paste is well mixed in. Add the stock or water and coconut milk and bring to a low boil, stirring. Put in the French beans and simmer for 3 minutes. Add the aubergines and simmer for another 3 minutes. Finally, add the cabbage and the salt and simmer until all the vegetables are just tender (another 5 minutes approximately). Serve.

Indonesian Fruit Salad (Rujak)

Serves 4

In this unusual fruit salad, fruits and vegetables are combined and served with a dressing made with chillies, vinegar and plenty of brown sugar. Use any combination of fresh fruit or vegetables in season. A selection is given below. Serve the fruit salad on its own or as part of a larger meal alongside savoury dishes, or as the last course of a lunch.

2 Granny Smith apples, peeled and
   cut into pieces
2 oranges, peeled, segmented
1 grapefruit, peeled, segmented
1/2 fresh pineapple, peeled and
   cubed *or* 1 small tin pineapple
1–2 firm mangoes, peeled and cut
   into pieces
1/2 cucumber, sliced
1 bunch radishes, washed, topped
   and tailed

Dressing

1 fresh *or* dried red chilli, seeds
   removed, finely chopped
1/2 teaspoon prawn paste, grilled
   (optional)
1 tablespoon dark soya sauce
4 oz (100 g) dark brown sugar
2 tablespoons white vinegar *or* 2
   tablespoons lemon juice

Combine all the fruits and vegetables in a large bowl. Mix together all
the dressing ingredients by hand or in a blender and then pour the
dressing over the fruit salad. Mix well and serve. The dressing can also
be served in individual bowls into which each fruit is dipped before
eating.

Fried Aubergines (Terung Goreng)

Serves 3–4

Serve as a side dish or with salad and rice as a light meal.

2 medium aubergines
salt
vegetable oil for frying
1 medium onion, finely sliced
paprika to taste

Slice the aubergines quite thickly, sprinkle the slices liberally with salt
and leave them in a colander to stand for 30 minutes. Rinse them under
cold water and dry on absorbent kitchen paper. Heat 3–4 tablespoons
of oil in a heavy frying pan or wok, and shallow fry the slices a few at a
time until lightly browned and cooked. Drain the fried slices on
absorbent paper. Meanwhile, fry the onion slices until crisp and
brown. Combine the aubergines and fried onion and season with salt
and paprika.

Aubergines and Tomatoes Cooked with Soya Sauce (Semur Terung Tomat)

Serves 4

Serve with boiled rice or as an accompaniment to other dishes.

2 medium aubergines, thickly
   sliced, each slice cut in half to
   form semicircles
salt
2 tablespoons vegetable oil
1 medium onion, sliced
2 cloves garlic, crushed

8 oz (225 g) ripe tomatoes peeled
   and chopped *or* tinned tomatoes,
   chopped
1/2 teaspoon chilli powder
2 tablespoons dark soya sauce
2 teaspoons dark brown sugar
salt and pepper to taste

Sprinkle the aubergines liberally with salt and leave them in a colander to stand for 30 minutes. Rinse them under cold water and dry them on absorbent kitchen paper. Heat the oil in a saucepan over a moderate heat and sauté the onion and garlic until the onion is softened. Add the aubergines and sauté for 2–3 minutes. Add the remaining ingredients and mix well. Cover the pan and simmer for 10 minutes, stirring occasionally. Adjust the seasoning and serve.

Cucumber Salad (Slada Ketimun)

Serves 4 as a side salad

There are two different dressings which you can use: Dressing 1 is lemon based and garlic flavoured while Dressing 2 is vinegar based and spiced with chilli powder.

1/2 medium cucumber, peeled,
   thinly sliced

Lemon Dressing
juice of 1 lemon
2 tablespoons vegetable oil
1 teaspoon sugar

2 cloves garlic, crushed
salt to taste

Chilli Dressing
2 tablespoons white vinegar
1 teaspoon sugar

1/4 teaspoon chilli powder
1–2 spring onions, finely chopped

Combine the ingredients of dressing 1 or 2 and toss the cucumber slices in the mixture. Chill and serve.

Watercress and Cucumber Salad (Slada Kangkung)

Serves 4 as a side salad

Follow the recipe for cucumber salad but add a small bunch of watercress. To prepare the watercress, pluck the green sprigs from the stalks, wash and drain them and use only the sprigs in the salad.

Spinach and Sweet Corn Salad (Sayur Bayem Jagung)

Serves 4 as a side dish

12 fl oz (350 ml) stock
1 medium onion, sliced
1 clove garlic, crushed
8-oz (225-g) tin sweet corn, drained
salt to taste

1 lb (450 g) spinach, discard damaged leaves, cut off the stems if the spinach is old and discard them. Cut into 2-in (5-cm) lengths

Heat the stock in a pan, add the onion, garlic and sweet corn and gently boil the mixture until the onion is just tender. Add salt to taste. Add the spinach, return the pan to the boil, reduce the heat and simmer for 3 minutes. Adjust the seasoning and serve immediately as one of the dishes to accompany boiled rice.

Variation: Add ½ teaspoon prawn paste (terasi) and/or ground ginger to the stock at the same time as the onion and garlic.

Carrot and Apple Salad (Slada Wortel)

Serves 4 as a side dish

juice of 1 lemon
2 tablespoons vegetable oil (sesame seed *or* peanut oil are best)
salt and black pepper to taste

8 oz (225 g) carrots, peeled and grated
8 oz (225 g) eating apples, grated

Combine the lemon juice and oil and season it with salt and black pepper to make the dressing. Combine the carrot and apple, toss the mixture in the dressing and serve at once.

Stir Fried Carrots (Wortel Tumis)

Serves 4 as a side dish

Also see the recipe for stir fried vegetables on page 130.

2 tablespoons vegetable oil
1 small onion, finely sliced *or* 4
   spring onions, chopped
1 clove garlic, crushed
8 oz (225 g) carrots, peeled, cut
   into matchsticks

1 tablespoon dark soya sauce
1 tablespoon water
pinch chilli powder
pinch ground ginger

Heat the oil in a wok or frying pan and stir fry the onion and garlic for
1 minute. Add the carrots and stir fry for a further minute. Add the
remaining ingredients and cook, stirring, for 2 minutes. You
shouldn't need to add salt as the soya sauce is salty. Serve immediately.

Variation: Other vegetables such as green beans, celery, cauliflower,
or cabbage can also be cooked this way.

Broccoli with Coconut Sauce
(Brokoli Bumbu Kelapa)

Serves 4 as a side dish

1 lb (450 g) broccoli
water
2 tablespoons vegetable oil
4 oz (100 g) desiccated *or* freshly
   grated coconut
1/2 medium onion, sliced
1 clove garlic, crushed

1 fresh *or* dried red chilli, chopped,
   seeds removed *or* 1/4 teaspoon
   chilli powder
juice of 1 lemon
3 tablespoons water
salt to taste

Remove any large leaves from the broccoli, cut off the stem ends and
divide any large heads into florets. Place the broccoli in a saucepan,
add 1/2 in (1 cm) water, add salt, cover and gently cook until tender
(10–15 minutes). Meanwhile, heat the oil in a frying pan and add the
coconut, onion, garlic and chilli. Stir fry until the coconut is browned
and the onion is softened. Put the mixture into the container of a
blender, add the lemon juice, water and salt and blend it to a smooth
sauce. Drain the broccoli, pour over the coconut sauce and serve.

Variation: Add 1/2 teaspoon prawn paste (terasi) or anchovy essence to
the mixture in the blender.

Spiced Stir Fried Green Beans (Buncis Tumis)

Serves 4 as a side dish

2 tablespoons vegetable oil
12 oz (350 g) French *or* green
   beans, topped, tailed and cut
   into 2-in (5-cm) pieces

1 small onion, finely diced
2 cloves garlic, crushed
1/2 teaspoon hot pepper sauce
1 tablespoon dark soya sauce

Heat the oil in a wok or frying pan and stir fry the beans, onion and garlic for 2–3 minutes. Add the hot pepper sauce and soya sauce and stir fry a further minute. Remove the pan from the heat and serve.

BEAN CURD AND BEAN CAKE DISHES
(Masakan Tahu Tempe)

Tahu and tempe are both made from soya beans. Tahu is known as bean curd in the West and is usually familiar to people who eat in Chinese restaurants. It is made from a liquid extracted from crushed soya beans and is soft in texture. Tahu is sold in small square slabs and is now quite widely available in the West. It is normally stored in water and will keep for 2–3 days in the refrigerator. Fried tahu has a yellow firm crust and is generally used in cooked dishes in which fresh tahu would break up. Fried tahu could be added to any of the mixed vegetable recipes given in this book. Tempe is made by combining soaked soya beans with an enzyme-producing agent such as yeast which breaks down the beans and then binds them together. By this action the beans are easier to digest. Tempe is sold in slabs in which the individual beans can be seen. The surface of the slabs develops a white skin similar to that found on some cheeses, like, for example, brie. The texture of tempe ranges from soft to crunchy and the taste is slightly nutty. Tempe is an excellent source of protein, vitamin, carbohydrate and minerals and it is an important nutritional food in South East Asia. As much as the Chinese are credited for discovering the process of making tahu thousands of years ago, the Indonesians must be credited for their genius in fermenting soya beans to make tempe.

I have given only a few recipes for tahu and tempe because, fresh or shallow fried or deep fried, cut into cubes, they could be added to almost any of the savoury recipes given in this book, especially the mixed vegetable dishes. Give them about 10–15 minutes cooking time in whichever recipe they are added. They absorb the flavour of the other ingredients and add goodness and interest to soups, gado-gado, salads and main meals.

Fried Tempe (Tempe Goreng)

Serves 4

Fried tempe is very nice served as a snack or side dish lightly sprinkled with salt or accompanied by a sambal dipping sauce (see pages 42–7). It is also the basic ingredient of the two tempe recipes that follow this one.

12 oz (350 g) tempe, cut into sticks about 2 in × ¼ in × ½ in (5 cm × 1 cm × ½ cm)

oil for deep frying
salt to taste

Heat the oil (about 1 in/2.5 cm deep) in a frying pan over a medium flame. Add half the tempe sticks and fry, stirring, until they turn golden brown, about 5 minutes. Remove them with a small sieve or slotted spoon and set them to drain on absorbent kitchen paper. Repeat for the remaining tempe. Combine the two batches of tempe, sprinkle with salt and serve.

Seasoned and Fried Tempe (Tempe Bumbu Goreng)

Serves 4

Ingredients as for fried tempe recipe above, plus:

2 cloves garlic, crushed
1 teaspoon salt
½ teaspoon freshly ground pepper
1 teaspoon ground coriander

4 fl oz (100 ml) water
juice of 1 lemon *or* 3 tablespoons tamarind water

Mix all the ingredients together in a bowl and add half the tempe sticks. Stir them about in the bowl to coat each stick with the seasoning. Leave to marinate for 5–10 minutes. Prepare a sieve over a bowl. Remove the sticks and set them to drain for a few minutes in the sieve. Deep fry the seasoned tempe as directed in the fried tempe recipe. Repeat for the remaining tempe.

Fried Tempe in Hot Sauce (Sambal Goreng Tempe)

Serves 4

Ingredients as for fried tempe recipe above, plus:

1 medium onion, finely chopped
2 cloves garlic
2 fresh *or* dried red chillies, seeded

2 fl oz (50 ml) water
2 teaspoons brown sugar
1 teaspoon salt

Fry the tempe sticks as directed in the fried tempe recipe and keep the fried sticks warm in a hot oven. Put the onion, garlic, chillies and water into a blender or food processor and blend them to a paste. Remove all but 2 tablespoons of oil from the frying pan in which the tempe was fried. Add the paste and stir fry it for 4–5 minutes. Stir in the sugar and salt and then the fried tempe. Mix well and serve immediately.

Fried Bean Curd (Tahu Goreng)

Serves 4

Fried bean curd is good both as a snack served on its own or with a sambal dipping sauce (see pages 42–7), or served with other dishes as part of a meal. It is also the basic ingredient of the three tahu recipes that follow this one.

4 cakes fresh, medium hard bean
    curd about 4 oz (100 g) each, cut
    into 1-in (2.5-cm) cubes
oil for deep frying
2 tablespoons dark soya sauce

To garnish

4 spring onions, finely chopped

Heat the oil (about 2 in/5 cm deep) in a frying pan and deep fry the bean curd cubes, a portion at a time, until crisp and golden brown on all sides. Remove them from the pan with a slotted spoon and drain on absorbent kitchen paper and place them on a serving dish. Pour over the soya sauce, garnish with chopped spring onions and serve.

Fried Bean Curd with Soya Sauce
(Tahu Goreng Kecap)

Serves 4

Ingredients as for fried bean curd recipe above, plus:

1 medium onion, chopped	2 fl oz (50 ml) dark soya sauce
1–2 fresh *or* dried red chillies	2 teaspoons lemon juice
2 cloves garlic	

Prepare the fried bean curd as described in the recipe above and keep it warm in a hot oven. Put the onion, chilli, garlic, soya sauce, and lemon juice into the container of a blender or food processor and blend the mixture to a smooth consistency. Transfer the sauce to a small pan and bring it to a gentle boil. Garnish the fried tempe with the chopped spring onions and then pour over the boiling sauce. Serve.

Seasoned and Fried Bean Curd
(Tahu Bumbu Goreng)

Serves 4

Ingredients as for fried bean curd recipe above, plus:

2 cloves garlic, crushed	*To garnish*
1 teaspoon salt	
1/2 teaspoon pepper	4 spring onions, chopped
4 fl oz (100 ml) tamarind water *or*	
juice of 1 lemon and 2 fl oz	
(50 ml) water	

Put the garlic, salt, pepper, tamarind water or lemon juice and water into a bowl and mix well. Dip one third of the tahu cubes in the bowl and stir them about. Lift them out with a slotted spoon and allow the excess liquid to drip back into the bowl. Deep fry the cubes as described in the fried bean curd recipe. Repeat for the remaining two portions of bean curd. Drain the fried bean curd on absorbent kitchen paper and serve garnished with spring onions.

Fried Bean Curd with Vegetables (Tahu Sayur Bumbu Kacang)

Serves 4

Ingredients as for fried bean curd recipe above, plus:

2 fl oz (50 ml) soya sauce
3 tablespoons crunchy peanut
   butter
2 cloves garlic
1–2 fresh *or* dried red chillies
2 tablespoons lemon juice

2 tablespoons water
1 teaspoon salt
4 oz (100 g) beansprouts
4 oz (100 g) cabbage, shredded
1/2 cucumber, peeled, seeded and
   diced

To garnish

4 spring onions, chopped

Fry the bean curd as directed in the fried bean curd recipe above and keep it warm in a hot oven. Put the soya sauce, peanut butter, garlic, chillies, lemon juice, water and salt into a blender or food processor and blend the mixture to a smooth consistency. Remove all but about 2 tablespoons of oil from the frying pan in which the bean curd was fried. Add the sauce and stir fry over a moderate heat for 4–5 minutes. Remove from the heat. Lightly blanch the beansprouts and cabbage separately in fast boiling water and drain them. Put the fried bean curd onto a serving dish, surround it with beansprouts and cabbage, sprinkle over the diced cucumber, cover with sauce and garnish with spring onions. Serve.

EGG DISHES
(Masakan Telur)

Both chicken and duck eggs are commonly used in Indonesian cooking in the same ways as they are in Western cooking – they are fried, boiled, and made into omelettes. They are also preserved but salt is used rather than vinegar. My host in Indonesia was keen for me to try a salted duck's egg but for some reason I was never very keen. One evening, after a large meal in which I had 'tried' too many dishes already, he looked at me, put his hand in his pocket and produced a salted duck's egg for me to try. I still haven't tasted one.

Below are recipes for a few Indonesian egg dishes. I have chosen them because they show Indonesian methods for preparing everyday egg dishes.

Indonesian Omelette (Omelet)

Serves 2–4

Two methods are given here. In the first the onion and chilli pepper are stir fried before the egg is added. In the second, all the ingredients are combined and cooked together and the onion remains quite crunchy. Serve the omelette if you wish with the omelette sauce for which a recipe is given on page 147. Method 1 makes one large omelette and method 2 makes two smaller ones.

2 tablespoons vegetable oil *or* 1 oz
  (25 g) butter
1 small onion, finely sliced

1–2 fresh *or* dried red chillies,
  finely sliced
4 eggs, beaten
salt and pepper to taste

Method 1

Heat the oil or butter in a heavy frying pan, add the onion and chilli pepper and fry until softened. Add salt and pepper to the beaten eggs and pour the mixture into the pan. Cook over a moderate heat until set and lightly browned on the bottom. Carefully turn the omelette over and brown the other side. Transfer the omelette to a serving dish and cut it into wedges before serving.

Method 2

Combine all the ingredients except the oil or butter and mix them well together. Heat a small or medium-sized heavy frying pan over a moderate heat, add half the oil or butter, heat it and then add half the egg mixture. Cook until the omelette is set and lightly browned on the bottom side. Turn the omelette over and brown the other side. Repeat for the remaining half of the mixture.

Soya Sauce Omelette (Omelet Kecap)

Serves 2–4

This is the Javanese way of flavouring omelettes. Follow method 1 above but instead of salt use 2 teaspoons of dark soya sauce. Add pepper to taste and then proceed as directed in the recipe.

Bean Curd Omelette (Tahu Telur)

Serves 4

Follow method 2 above but add a square of fresh bean curd cut into small pieces to the ingredients.

Prawn Omelette (Omelet Udang)

Serves 4

2 tablespoons vegetable oil *or* 1 oz (25 g) butter
1-in (2.5-cm) piece of root ginger, finely chopped
1 small onion, diced
1 clove garlic, crushed

8 oz (225 g) prawns, shelled and, if large, deveined, cut into pieces *or* use small tinned prawns, drained of any liquid
4 eggs, beaten
dark soya sauce to taste
pepper to taste

Heat the oil or butter in a frying pan and stir fry the ginger, onion and garlic in it for 1–2 minutes. Add the prawn pieces and stir fry until they are cooked. Season the beaten egg with dark soya sauce and pepper and add the mixture to the pan. Cook over a moderate heat until the omelette is set and just browned on the bottom side. Carefully turn the omelette over and cook the other side. Transfer it to a serving dish and cut it into wedges before serving.

Sauce for Omelettes (Saos Untuk Omelet)

1 tablespoon vegetable oil *or* butter
2 cloves garlic, crushed
1 small onion, diced
2 ripe tomatoes, chopped

1–2 fresh *or* dried red chillies, finely sliced
3 teaspoons dark soya sauce
2 tablespoons water
pepper to taste

Heat the oil or butter in a small pan and sauté the onion and garlic until softened. Add the remaining ingredients and cook the mixture over a moderate heat until the tomatoes have disintegrated. Pour the sauce over the omelette and serve.

Variation: Replace the tomatoes by 4 tablespoons crunchy peanut butter and proceed as directed in the recipe.

Quick Fried Cabbage with Eggs (Orak Arik)

Serves 2–4

1 tablespoon vegetable oil
1 medium onion, finely sliced
8 oz (225 g) cabbage *or* Chinese cabbage, finely shredded

salt and pepper to taste
pinch of chilli powder
2 eggs, beaten

Heat the oil in a heavy frying pan or wok and fry the onion in it until softened. Add the cabbage, salt and pepper and a pinch of chilli powder. Stir fry for 2–3 minutes and then cover the pan and cook the mixture over a low heat for 10 minutes. Now stir in the beaten eggs and scramble them with the cabbage. As soon as the egg has set, serve.

Variation: Add 6 oz (175 g) of tinned crab meat and shredded or tinned prawns, drained, to the beaten eggs before adding to the pan.

Hard-boiled Eggs with Sauce

Serves 4–6

Hard boil 4–6 eggs, shell and halve them. Make one of the two sauces given below, put the eggs in and heat them through for 3–4 minutes, spooning the sauce over the eggs. Serve as a side dish or with vegetables and rice as a light meal. Alternatively, leave the eggs to marinate in the sauce for 1–2 hours, reheat and serve as above.

Soya Sauce (Telur Pindang)

2 tablespoons vegetable oil
1 small onion, finely sliced
1 clove garlic, crushed
1–2 fresh *or* dried chillies, seeded
 and finely sliced

2 medium ripe tomatoes, skinned
 and chopped
1/2 teaspoon ground ginger
1 tablespoon dark brown sugar
1 tablespoon white vinegar
4 fl oz (100 ml) water

Heat the oil in a saucepan and sauté the onion, garlic and chillies until the onion is softened. Add the tomatoes and ground ginger and cook, stirring, until the tomato has pulped. Add the remaining ingredients, bring the mixture to the boil, stir it well, cover, reduce the heat and simmer for 5 minutes. It is now ready.

Chilli and Tomato Sauce (Belado Telur)

3 tablespoons vegetable oil
1 medium onion, finely sliced
1–2 teaspoons chilli powder *or* hot
 pepper sauce

8 oz (225 g) ripe tomatoes, peeled
 and chopped
1 teaspoon white sugar
salt to taste
juice of 1/2 lemon

Heat the oil in a saucepan, add the onion and sauté it until it is lightly browned. Add the chilli powder or hot pepper sauce, tomatoes and sugar and cook, stirring, until the tomatoes have pulped. Season with salt and lemon juice. Mix well and simmer the sauce, uncovered, for 5 minutes. It is now ready.

SPECIAL NOTES FOR
AMERICAN COOKS

As all measurements are given in imperial and metric a table of cup conversion measurements for ingredients commonly used in this book is given below. The following list of cooking terms and ingredients used in the text, with their American equivalents, is given to help clarify the text.

English	*American*
plain flour	white flour
aubergine	eggplant
chilli powder	chilli seasoning
cooking fat	shortening
cornflour	cornstarch
courgette	zucchini
desiccated coconut	shredded coconut
frying pan	skillet
to grill	to broil
hard-boiled egg	hard-cooked egg
king prawns	jumbo shrimps
minced	ground
pinch of	dash of
to sieve	to strain
spring onion	scallion
stone or seed	pit
to shell	to hull
tin	can

ENGLISH/AMERICAN CUP
CONVERSION TABLE

English	American
6 oz bamboo shoot, tinned, sliced	1 cup
6 oz banana, 1 medium, sliced	1 cup
8 oz butter	1 cup
4 oz cabbage, shredded	1 cup
3 oz coconut, desiccated	1 cup
4 oz flour, plain	1 cup
2 oz herbs, chopped	1 cup
lemon, 1 medium	{ 2 US tablespoons juice / 1 teaspoon grated rind
8 oz meat, in 1-in (2.5-cm) cubes	1 cup
10 oz mincemeat, finely minced	1 cup
4 oz nuts, coarsely chopped	1 cup
8 fl oz oil	1 cup
5 oz onion, chopped	1 cup
4 oz peanuts, raw	1 cup
8 oz peanut butter	1 cup
6 oz rice, uncooked	1 cup
5 oz sugar, brown	1 cup
4 oz tomato, 1 medium, chopped	1 cup
4 oz (approx.) vegetables, diced or matchstick	1 cup

WEIGHTS AND MEASURES
METRIC/IMPERIAL CONVERSION TABLE

Ounces/fluid ounces (oz/fl oz)	Grammes or millilitres (g/ml) (to the nearest unit of 25)
1	25
2	50
3	75
4	100
5	150
6	175
7	200
8	225
9	250
10	275
11	300
12	350
13	375
14	400
15	425
16	450
17	475
18	500
19	550
20	575

AMERICAN/IMPERIAL/METRIC

1 American tablespoon = 2 English teaspoons = 1/2 English tablespoon
1 American teaspoon = 5-ml metric spoon
1 American tablespoon = 15-ml metric spoon
2 American or metric tablespoons (1/8 cup) = 1 fl oz = approx. 25 ml
1 1/4 American pints = 1 English pint = 20 fl oz = 550 ml
1 American pint = 3/4 English pint = 16 fl oz = 450 ml
1 American pint = 2 cups
2 1/5 American pints = 1 3/4 English pints = 1 litre

OVEN TEMPERATURES

°F	°C	Gas Mark
225	110	1/4
250	130	1/2
275	140	1
300	150	2
325	170	3
350	180	4
375	190	5
400	200	6
425	225	7
450	230	8
475	240	9

INDEX